D1506452

THE TEARS OF CHRIST

Meditations for Lent

THE TEARS OF CHRIST

Meditations for Lent

St. John Henry Newman

Edited by
Christopher O. Blum

Augustine Institute
Greenwood Village, CO

Augustine Institute
6160 S. Syracuse Way
Greenwood Village, CO 80111
Tel: (866) 767-3155
www.augustineinstitute.org

Cover design by Lisa Marie Patterson

Printed in Canada

CONTENTS

Third Week of Lent

Fourth Week of Lent

Fifth Week of Lent

Holy Week

Solemnities of the Lenten Season

Introduction

"Jesus wept, not merely from the deep thoughts of his understanding but from spontaneous tenderness, from the goodness and mercy, the encompassing loving-kindness and exuberant affection of the Son of God for his own work, the race of man."[1] This precious insight takes us to the heart of the interior life of St. John Henry Newman (1801–1890), from the treasures of which these meditations are offered as a devotional aid for the season of Lent.

To the first-time reader of Newman, it may come as a surprise that these passages have been drawn from his sermons, and chiefly those preached while he was a clergyman in the Church of England. Even during his Anglican years, Newman's spiritual vision was remarkably Catholic, such that his decision to become a Roman Catholic in 1845 was very much in harmony with his earlier life. From his youthful studies at Oxford University he had nourished a love for the writings of the Fathers of the Church, whose example and teaching led him ineluctably to the fullness of the faith. Readers of his various writings but especially of his "many fine sermons" can easily appreciate why Benedict XVI numbered him among the "saints and scholars" of Catholic England who have given the Church such a valuable witness of "gentle scholarship, deep human wisdom and profound love for the Lord."[2]

---

[1] "The Tears of Christ," below at page 144.
[2] Benedict XVI, "Homily for the Beatification of John Henry Cardinal Newman," 19 September 2010. Available at Vatican.va.

Monsignor Ronald Knox, himself a convert from the Church of England, once observed that "in ordinary Anglican churches the sermon is the climax, not an interlude as it is at [Roman Catholic] High Mass."[3] The typical Catholic homily today is a brief exhortation delivered from memory and constrained by the parishioners' expectation that Mass end on time. In marked contrast, Newman's Anglican sermons were anywhere from forty to sixty minutes in length and were delivered from carefully prepared texts the wisdom and eloquence of which were celebrated during his lifetime. In this volume, as in its companion *Waiting for Christ: Meditations for Advent and Christmas* (Augustine Institute, 2018), selections from Newman's sermons are presented in a gently modernized form. Other than to select shorter passages from the longer originals, the principal editorial changes have been to replace quotations from the King James Version of the Bible with those from the Revised Standard Version, Second Catholic Edition, and to have adjusted the flow of the text by updating Newman's punctuation. Let the reader be assured that the thoughts here presented are entirely Newman's own, and that the verbal changes that have been made to the texts are very few in number.

Like all great preachers, St. John Henry Newman spent countless hours reading and contemplating Scripture, especially the four Gospels. In these selections from his sermons, we can share in the fruit of his contemplation, that we might the better enjoy with him the "one thing which is all in all to us," which is "to live in Christ's presence, to hear his voice, to see his countenance."[4] We may join in prayer with Newman that,

---

[3] Monsignor Ronald Knox, *A Spiritual Aeneid (Westminster, Maryland: The Newman Press, 1948)*, 28.

[4] "Apostolic Abstinence a Pattern for Christians," below at page 99.

through our Lenten devotions, God will give us "the beauty of holiness, which consists in tender and eager affection towards our Lord and Savior, so that through God's mercy our souls may have not strength and health only but a sort of bloom and comeliness, and that as we grow older in body, we may, year by year, grow more youthful in spirit."[5]

Christopher O. Blum
Augustine Institute
Greenwood Village, Colorado
Feast of St. Philip Neri, 2019

---

[5] "The Crucifixion," below at page 189.

Ash Wednesday

The Cross of Christ, the Measure of the World, I

A great number of men live and die without reflecting at all upon the state of things in which they find themselves. They take things as they come and follow their inclinations as far as they have the opportunity. They are guided mainly by pleasure and pain, not by reason, principle, or conscience, and they do not attempt to interpret this world, to determine what it means, or to reduce what they see and feel to system. But when persons begin to contemplate the visible state of things into which they are born, they find it a maze and a perplexity. It is a riddle which they cannot solve.

In this difficulty, some have formed one philosophy of life and others another. Men have thought they had found the key by means of which they might read what is so obscure. Ten thousand things come before us, one after another, in the course of life, and what are we to think of them? Are we to look at all things in a desponding or a hopeful way? Are we to make light of life altogether or to treat the whole subject seriously? Are we to make greatest things of little consequence or least things of great consequence? Are we to keep in mind what is past and gone, or are we to look on to the future, or are we to be absorbed in what is present? How are we to look at things? This is the question which all persons of observation ask themselves, and answer each in his own way. They wish to think by rule, by something within them which may harmonize and adjust what is without them. What is the real key, what is the Christian interpretation of this world? What is given us by revelation to estimate and measure this world by? It is the event of this season: the Crucifixion of the Son of God.

It is the death of the Eternal Word of God made flesh which is our great lesson how to think and how to speak of this world. His Cross has put its due value upon everything which we see, upon all fortunes, all advantages, all ranks, all dignities, all pleasures, upon the lust of the flesh, and the lust of the eyes, and the pride of life (see 1 Jn 2:16). It has set a price upon the excitements, the rivalries, the hopes, the fears, the desires, the efforts, the triumphs of mortal man. It has given a meaning to the shifting course, the trials, the temptations, the sufferings, of his earthly state. It has brought together and made consistent all that seemed discordant and aimless. It has taught us how to live, how to use this world, what to expect, what to desire, what to hope. It is the tone into which all the strains of this world's music are ultimately to be resolved.

Look around and see what the world presents of high and low. Go to the court of princes. See the treasure and skill of all nations brought together to honor a child of man. Consider the form and ceremonial, the pomp, the circumstance, and the vainglory. Do you wish to know the worth of it all? Look at the Cross of Christ.

Go to the political world. See nation jealous of nation, trade rivalling trade, armies and fleets matched against each other. Survey the various ranks of the community, its parties and their contests, the strivings of the ambitious, the intrigues of the crafty. What is the end of all this turmoil? The grave. What is the measure? The Cross.

Go, again, to the world of intellect and science. Consider the wonderful discoveries which the human mind is making, the variety of arts to which its discoveries give rise, the all but miracles by which it shows its power, the pride and confidence of reason, and the absorbing devotion of thought to transitory objects which is the consequence. Would you form a right judgment of all this? Look at the Cross.

Again, look at misery, look at poverty and destitution, look at oppression and captivity; go where food is scanty, and lodging unhealthy. Consider pain and suffering, diseases long or violent, all that is frightful and revolting. Would you know how to rate all these? Gaze upon the Cross.

In the Cross, and him who hung upon it, all things meet. It is their center and their interpretation. For he was lifted up upon it, that he might draw all men and all things unto himself.

But it will be said that the view which the Cross of Christ imparts to us of human life and of the world is not that which we should take, if left to ourselves; that it is not an obvious view; that if we look at things on their surface, they are far more bright and sunny. The world seems made for the enjoyment of just such a being as man, and man is put into it. How natural this, what a simple as well as pleasant philosophy, yet how different from that of the Cross! The doctrine of the Cross, it may be said, disarranges two parts of a system which seem made for each other; it severs the fruit from the eater, the enjoyment from the enjoyer. How does this solve a problem? Does it not rather itself create one?

Whatever force this objection may have, surely it is merely a repetition of that which Eve felt and Satan urged in Eden. For did not the woman see that the forbidden tree was "good for food" and a tree "to be desired"? (Gen 3:6). Well, then, is it wonderful that we too, the descendants of the first pair, should still be in a world where there is a forbidden fruit, and that our trials should lie in being within reach of it and our happiness in abstaining from it? The world, at first sight, appears made for pleasure, and the vision of Christ's Cross is a solemn and sorrowful sight interfering with this appearance. Be it so. But why may it not be our duty to abstain from enjoyment notwithstanding, if it was a duty even in Eden?

The doctrine of the Cross does but teach—though infinitely more forcibly—the very same lesson which this world teaches to those who live long in it, who have much experience in it, who know it. The world is sweet to the lips, but bitter to the taste. It pleases at first, but not at last. When a man has passed a certain number of years in it, he cries out with the Preacher, "Vanity of vanities . . . all is vanity" (Eccles 1:2). Nay, if he has not religion for his guide, he will be forced to go further, and say all is disappointment; all is sorrow; all is pain. The sore judgments of God upon sin are concealed within it and force a man to grieve whether he will or no. Therefore, the doctrine of the Cross of Christ does but anticipate for us our experience of the world. It is true, it bids us grieve for our sins in the midst of all that smiles and glitters around us, but if we will not heed it, we shall at length be forced to grieve for them from undergoing their fearful punishment. If we will not acknowledge that this world has been made miserable by sin, from the sight of him on whom our sins were laid, we shall experience it to be miserable by the recoil of those sins upon ourselves.

Thursday after Ash Wednesday

The Cross of Christ, the Measure of the World, II

The doctrine of the Cross is not on the surface of the world. The surface of things is bright only, and the Cross is sorrowful. It is a hidden doctrine; it lies under a veil. At first sight, it startles us, and we are tempted to revolt from it. Like St. Peter, we cry out, "God forbid, Lord! This shall never happen to you" (Mt 16:22). Yet it is a true doctrine, for truth is not on the surface of things, but in the depths.

And as the doctrine of the Cross, though it be the true interpretation of this world, is not prominently manifested upon its surface but is concealed, so again, when received into the faithful heart, it abides as a living principle, but deep and hidden from observation. Religious men, in the words of Scripture, "live by the faith of the Son of God, who loved" them and gave himself for them (see Gal 2:20), but they do not tell this to all men. They leave others to find it out as they may. Our Lord's own command to his disciples was that when they fast they should "anoint" their head and "wash" their face (Mt 6:17). They are bound not to make a display but ever to be content to look outwardly different from what they are inwardly. They are to carry a cheerful countenance with them and to control and regulate their feelings, that those feelings, by not being expended on the surface, may retire deep into their hearts and there live. And thus "Jesus Christ and him crucified" (1 Cor 2:2) is, as the apostle tells us, a "hidden wisdom" (1 Cor 2:7), hidden in the world, which seems at first sight to speak a far other doctrine, and hidden in the faithful soul, which to persons at a distance, or to chance beholders, seems to be living but an ordinary life, while really it is in secret holding communion with him who was "manifested in the flesh, vindicated in the Spirit, seen by angels," and "taken up in glory" (1 Tim 3:16).

This being the case, the great and awful doctrine of the Cross of Christ may be called the heart of religion. The heart may be considered as the seat of life. It sustains the man in his powers and faculties, and when it is touched, man dies. In like manner, the sacred doctrine of Christ's atoning sacrifice is the vital principle on which the Christian lives, and without which Christianity is not. Without it no other doctrine is held profitably. To believe in Christ's divinity, or in his manhood, or in the Holy Trinity, or in a judgment to come is an untrue belief, unless we receive also the doctrine of Christ's sacrifice. Yet to receive it presupposes the reception of other high truths of the Gospel besides: it involves the belief in Christ's true divinity, in his true incarnation, and in man's sinful state by nature. And it prepares the way to belief in the sacred eucharistic feast, in which he who was once crucified is ever given to our souls and bodies in his Body and Blood.

It must not be supposed, because the doctrine of the Cross makes us sad, that therefore the Gospel is a sad religion. The Psalmist says, "Those who sow in tears reap with shouts of joy" (Ps 126:5); and our Lord says, those who mourn "shall be comforted" (Mt 5:4). Let no one go away with the impression that the Gospel makes us take a gloomy view of the world and of life. It hinders us indeed from taking a superficial view and finding a vain transitory joy in what we see, but it forbids our immediate enjoyment only to grant enjoyment in truth and fullness afterwards. It only says, if you begin with pleasure, you will end with pain. It bids us begin with the Cross of Christ, and in that Cross we shall at first find sorrow, but in a while peace and comfort will rise out of that sorrow. That Cross will lead us to mourning, repentance, humiliation, prayer, fasting. We shall sorrow for our sins, we shall sorrow with Christ's sufferings. But all this sorrow will be undergone in a happiness far greater than the enjoyment which the world gives—though careless worldly minds indeed will not believe this, will ridicule the notion of it and consider it a mere matter of words which no one really feels. This is what they think. But our Savior said to his disciples, "you have sorrow now, but I will see you again and your hearts will rejoice, and no one will take your joy from you" (Jn 16:22). "Peace I leave with you; my peace I give to you; not as the world gives do I give to you" (Jn 14:27). And St. Paul says, "What no eye has seen, nor ear heard, nor the heart of man conceived . . . God has prepared for those who love him" (1 Cor 2:9). And thus the Cross of Christ, as telling us of our redemption as well as of his sufferings, wounds us indeed, but so wounds as to heal also.

And thus, too, all that is bright and beautiful, even on the surface of this world, though it has no substance and may not suitably be enjoyed for its own sake, yet is a figure and promise of that true joy which issues out of the atonement. It is a promise beforehand of what is to be. It is a shadow, raising hope because the substance is to follow, but not to be rashly taken instead of the substance. And it is God's usual mode of dealing with us, in mercy to send the shadow before the substance, that we may take comfort in what is to be before it comes. Thus, our Lord before his Passion rode into Jerusalem in triumph, with the multitudes crying Hosanna and strewing his road with palm branches and their garments. This was but a vain and hollow pageant, nor did our Lord take pleasure in it. It was a shadow which stayed not but flitted away. It could not be more than a shadow, for the Passion had not been undergone by which his true triumph was accomplished. He could not enter into his glory before he had first suffered. He could not take pleasure in this semblance of it, knowing that it was unreal. Yet that first shadowy triumph was the omen and presage of the true victory to come, when he had overcome the sharpness of death.

And so, too, as regards this world, with all its enjoyments, yet disappointments. Let us not trust it. Let us not give our hearts to it. Let us not begin with it. Let us begin with Christ. Let us begin with his Cross and the humiliation to which it leads. Let us first be drawn to him who is lifted up, that he may, with himself, freely give us all things. Let us "seek first his kingdom and his righteousness," and then all those things of this world shall be ours as well (Mt 6:33). They alone are able truly to enjoy this world who begin with the world unseen. They alone enjoy it who have first abstained from it. They alone inherit it who take it as a shadow of the world to come, and who for that world to come relinquish it.

Friday after Ash Wednesday

Fasting a Source of Trial

The season of humiliation which precedes Easter lasts for forty days in memory of our Lord's long fast in the wilderness. We fast by way of penitence and to subdue the flesh. Our Savior had no need of fasting for either purpose. His fasting was unlike ours, as in its intensity, so in its object. And yet when we begin to fast, his pattern is set before us, and we continue the time of fasting till in number of days we have equaled his.

There is a reason for this: we must do nothing except with him in our eye. As he it is, through whom alone we have the power to do any good thing, so unless we do it for him it is not good. From him our obedience comes, towards him it must look. He says, "apart from me you can do nothing" (Jn 15:5). No work is good without grace and without love.

Even in our penitential exercises, Christ has gone before us to sanctify them to us. He has blessed fasting as a means of grace, in that he has fasted, and fasting is only acceptable when it is done for his sake. Penitence is mere formality, or mere remorse, unless done in love. If we fast without uniting ourselves in heart to Christ, imitating him, and praying that he would make our fasting his own and communicate to it the virtue of his own, then we beat the air and humble ourselves in vain.

It is commonly said that fasting is intended to make us better Christians, to sober us, and to bring us more entirely at Christ's feet in faith and humility. On the whole, this effect will be produced, but it is not at all certain that it will follow at once.

Mortifications have various effects on different persons. Some men, indeed, are subdued by fasting and brought at once nearer to God; but others find it, however slight, scarcely more than an occasion of temptation. For instance, it is sometimes even made an objection to fasting, as if it were a reason for not practicing it, that it makes a man irritable and ill-tempered. Again, what very often follows from it is a feebleness which deprives him of his command over his bodily acts, feelings, and expressions. Weakness of body may deprive him of self-command in other ways; perhaps weakness of body hinders him from fixing his mind on his prayers instead of making him pray more fervently. Or again, weakness of body is often attended with languor and listlessness and strongly tempts a man to sloth.

Yet the most distressing of the effects which may follow from even the moderate exercise of this great Christian duty is that it is undeniably a means of temptation. And the merciful Lord knows that it is so from experience; and that he has experienced and thus knows it, as Scripture records, is to us a thought full of comfort. And, perhaps, this is the truest view of such exercises, that in some wonderful unknown way they open the next world for good and evil upon us and are an introduction to somewhat of an extraordinary conflict with the powers of evil. Stories are afloat of hermits in the deserts being assaulted by Satan in strange ways, yet resisting the evil one, and chasing him away, after our Lord's pattern and in his strength. And, if we knew the secret history of men's minds in any age, we should find a remarkable union in the case of those who by God's grace have made advances in holy things, a union on the one hand of temptations offered to the mind, and on the other, of the mind's not being affected by them, not consenting to them, even in momentary acts of the will, but simply hating them and receiving no harm from them. So far persons are evidently brought into fellowship and conformity with Christ, who was tempted, yet without sin.

Let it not then distress Christians, even if they find themselves exposed to thoughts from which they turn with abhorrence and terror. Rather let such a trial bring before their thoughts, with something of vividness and distinctness, the condescension of the Son of God. Certainly, it is a trial to us to have motives and feelings imputed to us before men, by the accuser of the brethren, which we never entertained. It is a trial to have ideas secretly suggested within, from which we shrink. It is a trial to us for Satan to be allowed so to mix his own thoughts with ours, that we feel guilty even when we are not; nay, to be able to set on fire our irrational nature, till in some sense we really sin against our will. But has not one gone before us more awful in his trial, more glorious in his victory? He "has been tempted as we are, yet without sinning" (Heb 4:15). Surely here too Christ's temptation speaks comfort and encouragement to us.

"He will give his angels charge of you to guard you in all your ways" (Ps 91:11); and the devil knows of this promise, for he used it in that very hour of temptation. He knows full well what our power is, and what is his own weakness. We have nothing to fear while we remain within the shadow of the throne of the Almighty. While we are found in Christ, we are partakers of his security. He has broken the power of Satan; "the lion and the adder; the young lion and the serpent" he has trampled underfoot (Ps 91:13), and henceforth evil spirits, instead of having power over us, tremble at every true Christian. They know he has that in him which makes him their master, that he may, if he will, laugh them to scorn and put them to flight. Sin alone gives them power over him, and their great object is to make him sin and therefore to surprise him into sin, knowing they have no other way of overcoming him. They try to scare him by the appearance of danger, or they approach stealthily and covertly to seduce him. But except by taking him at unawares, they can do nothing. Therefore, let us be "not ignorant of their devices" (2 Cor 2:11 KJV), and as knowing them, let us watch, fast, and pray. Let us keep close under the wings of the Almighty that he may be our shield and buckler. Let us pray him to make known to us his will, to teach us our faults, to take away whatever may offend him, and to lead us in the way everlasting. And during this sacred season, let us look upon ourselves as being on the mount with him, within the veil, hid with him, not out of him or apart from him in whose presence alone is life, but with and in him, learning of his law with Moses and of his attributes with Elijah and of his counsels with Daniel, learning to repent, learning to confess and to amend, learning his love and his fear, unlearning ourselves and growing up unto him who is our head.

Saturday after Ash Wednesday

The Yoke of Christ

Our Savior first calls us to him and next shows us the way. "Come to me," he says, "and I will give you rest," and then adds, "Take my yoke upon you and learn from me . . . and you will find rest for your souls" (Mt 11:28-9). He told the apostles that they must come to him but did not at once tell them the way. He told them they must bear a yoke but did not at once tell them what it was. St. Peter, in consequence, inquired about it on one occasion, and was bid to wait awhile, and he should know of it more plainly. Our Lord had said, "Where I am going you cannot follow me now; but you shall follow afterward" (Jn 13:36). "You will seek me," he said, but "where I am going you cannot come" (Jn 13:33). He spoke of his yoke, the way of his cross, as St. Peter found when at length, after the resurrection, he was told plainly what should befall him. "When you were young," said our Lord to him, when you were a child in the faith, and had your own way, "you fastened your own belt and walked where you would," as just before St. Peter had belted his fisher's coat unto him, and cast himself into the sea; "but when you are old, you will stretch out your hands, and another will fasten your belt for you and carry you where you do not wish to go." And then he added, "Follow me" (Jn 21:18-19).

St. Peter, indeed, was called upon literally to take Christ's yoke upon him, to learn of him and walk in his ways, but what he underwent in fullness, all Christ's disciples must share in their measure, in some way or other. In another place, our

Lord speaks more expressly: "If any man would come after me, let him deny himself and take up his cross and follow me" (Mt 16:24). To come to Christ is to come after him. To take up our cross is to take upon us his yoke. And though he calls this an easy yoke, yet it is easy because it is his yoke, and he makes it easy. Still it does not cease to be a yoke, and it is troublesome and distressing because it is a yoke.

All of us must come to Christ, in some sense or other, through things naturally unpleasant to us. It may be even through bodily suffering, such as the apostles endured, or it may be nothing more than the subduing of our natural infirmities and the sacrifice of our natural wishes. It may be pain greater or pain less, on a public stage or a private one, but, till the words "yoke" and "cross" can stand for something pleasant, the bearing of our yoke and cross is something not pleasant. And though rest is promised as our reward, yet the way to rest must lie through discomfort and distress of heart. This does not mean, far from it, that religion is not full of joy and peace also. "My yoke," says Christ, "is easy, and my burden is light" (Mt 11:30), but grace makes it so. In itself it is severe, and any form of doctrine which teaches otherwise forgets that Christ calls us to his yoke, and that that yoke is a cross.

One and the same character is acceptable to God, but unacceptable to man—unacceptable to man both in itself and because it involves a change, and that a painful one, in one shape or other. Nothing short of suffering, except in rare cases, makes us what we should be: gentle instead of harsh, meek instead of violent, conceding instead of arrogant, lowly instead of proud, pure-hearted instead of sensual, sensitive of sin instead of carnal. This is the object which is set before us: to become holy as he who has called us is holy and to discipline and chasten ourselves in order that we may become so. And we may be quite sure that, unless we chasten ourselves, God will chasten us. If we judge ourselves, through his mercy we shall not be judged of him. If we do not afflict ourselves in light things, he will afflict us in heavy things. If we do not set about changing ourselves by gentle measures, he will change us by severe remedies. "I pommel my body and subdue it," says St. Paul (1 Cor 9:27). Of course, Satan will try to turn all our attempts to his own purposes. He will try to make us think too much of ourselves for what we do. Of course, he turns all things to evil, as far as he can. All our crosses may become temptations. Illness, affliction, bereavement, pain, loss of worldly prospects, anxiety: all may be instruments of evil. So likewise may all methods of self-chastisement, but they ought not to be, and need not. And their legitimate effect, through the grace of the Holy Spirit, is to make us like him who suffered all pain, physical and moral, sin excepted, in its fullness. We know what his character was: how grave and subdued his speech, his manner, his acts; what calmness, self-possession, tenderness, and endurance; how he resisted evil; how he turned his cheek to the smiter; how he blessed when persecuted; how he resigned himself to his God and Father, how he suffered silently, and opened not his mouth, when accused maliciously.

There is but one cross and one character of mind formed by it.

If Almighty God moves any of us, so that it is given us to recognize the glory of Christ's kingdom, to discern its spiritual nature, to admire the life of saints, and to desire to imitate it; if we feel and understand that it is good to bear the yoke in our youth, good to be poor, good to be in low estate, good to be despised; if in imagination we put ourselves at the feet of those mortified men of old time, who, after St. Paul's pattern, died daily, and knew no one after the flesh; if we feel all this, and are conscious we feel it, let us not boast—why? Because of a surety such feelings are a pledge to us that God will in some way or other give them exercise. He gives them to us that he may use them. He gives us the opportunity of using them. Dare not to indulge in high thoughts. Be cautious of them, and refrain. They are the shadows of coming trials. They are not given for nothing; they are given for an end, and that end is coming. Never does God give faith, but he tries it. Never does he implant the wish to sit on his right hand and on his left, but he fulfils it by making us wash our brethren's feet.

First Sunday in Lent

Surrender to God

The strictness and severity in religion of former ages has been much relaxed. There has been a gradual abandonment of painful duties which were formerly enforced upon all. Time was when all persons, to speak generally, abstained from flesh through the whole of Lent. There have been dispensations on this point again and again. What is the meaning of this? What are we to gather from it?

Fasting is only one branch of a large and momentous duty, the subduing of ourselves to Christ. We must surrender to him all we have, all we are. We must keep nothing back. We must present to him as captive prisoners with whom he may do what he will, our soul and body, our reason, our judgment, our affections, our imagination, our tastes, our appetite. The great thing is to subdue ourselves, but as to the particular form in which the great precept of self-conquest and self-surrender is to be expressed, that depends on the person himself and on the time or place.

It follows that you must not suppose that nothing is incumbent on us in the way of mortification, though you have not to fast so strictly as formerly. It is reasonable to think that some other duty of the same general kind may take its place, and, therefore, the permission granted us in eating may be a suggestion to us to be more severe with ourselves in certain other respects.

This anticipation is confirmed by the history of our Lord's temptation in the wilderness. It began with an attempt on the part of the evil one to make him break his fast improperly. It began, but it did not end there. It was but the first of three temptations, and the other two were more addressed to his mind, not his bodily wants. One was to throw himself down from the pinnacle, the other the offer of all the kingdoms of the world. They were more subtle temptations. Everyone knows what it is to break the Ten Commandments, the first, the second, the third, and so on. When a thing is directly commanded, and the devil tempts us directly to break it, this is not a subtle temptation, but a broad and gross temptation. But there are a great many things wrong which are not so obviously wrong. They are wrong as leading to what is wrong or the consequence of what is wrong, or they are wrong because they are the very same thing as what is forbidden but dressed up and looking differently. The human mind is very deceitful. When a thing is forbidden, a man does not like directly to do it, but he goes to work if he can to get at the forbidden end in some way. It is like a sailing vessel at sea with the wind contrary, but tacking first this way, and then that, the mariners contrive at length to get to their destination. This then is a subtle sin, when it at first seems not to be a sin but comes round to the same point as an open direct sin.

A civilized age is more exposed to subtle sins than a rude age. Why? For this simple reason, because it is more fertile in excuses and evasions. It can defend error and hence can blind the eyes of those who have not very careful consciences. It can make error plausible; it can make vice look like virtue. It dignifies sin by fine names. It calls avarice proper care of one's family, or industry. It calls pride independence. It calls ambition greatness of mind. Resentment it calls proper spirit and sense of honor, and so on.

What all of us want more than anything else, what this age wants, is that its intellect and its will should be under a law.

At present it is lawless, its will is its own law, its own reason is the standard of all truth. It does not bow to authority, it does not submit to the law of faith. It is wise in its own eyes and relies on its own resources. And you, as living in the world, are in danger of being seduced by it, and being a partner in its sin, and so coming in at the end for its punishment. Now then let me suggest one or two points in which you may profitably subdue your minds, which require it even more than your bodies.

For example, in respect to curiosity. The desire of knowledge is in itself praiseworthy, but it may be excessive, it may take us from higher things, it may take up too much of our time: it is a vanity. "Of making many books there is no end, and much study is a weariness of the flesh. The end of the matter; all has been heard. Fear God, and keep his commandments; for this is the whole duty of man" (Eccles 12:12-3). Knowledge is very well in its place, but it is like flowers without fruit. We cannot feed on knowledge, we cannot thrive on knowledge. Just as the leaves of the grove are very beautiful but would make a bad meal, so we shall ever be hungry and never be satisfied if we think to take knowledge for our food. Knowledge is no food. Religion is our only food. Mortify your desire of knowledge. Do not go into excess in seeking after truths which are not religious.

Again, mortify your reason. In order to try you, God puts before you things which are difficult to believe. St. Thomas's faith was tried; so is yours. He said, "My Lord and my God" (Jn 20:28). You say so too. Bring your proud intellect into subjection. Believe what you cannot see, what you cannot understand, what you cannot explain, what you cannot prove, when God says it.

Finally, bring your will into subjection. We all like our own will; let us consult the will of others. Numbers of persons are obliged to do this. Servants are obliged to do the will of their masters, workmen of their employers, children of their parents, husbands of their wives. Well, in these cases, let your will go with that of those who have a right to command you. Don't rebel against it. Sanctify what is after all a necessary act. Make it in a certain sense your own, sanctify it, and get merit from it. And again, when you are your own master, be on your guard against going too much by your own opinion. Take some wise counsellor or director and obey him.

Monday of the First Week of Lent

The Duty of Self-Denial

Self-denial of some kind or other is involved in the very notion of renewal and holy obedience. To change our hearts is to learn to love things which we do not naturally love, to unlearn the love of this world. But this involves a thwarting of our natural wishes and tastes. To be righteous and obedient implies self-command. But to possess power we must have gained it, nor can we gain it without a vigorous struggle, a persevering warfare against ourselves. The very notion of being religious implies self-denial, because by nature we do not love religion.

Fasting is clearly a Christian duty, as our Savior implies in his Sermon on the Mount. Now what is fasting but a refraining from what is lawful, from that bread which we might lawfully take and eat with thanksgiving, but which at certain times we do not take, in order to deny ourselves? Such is Christian self-denial: not merely a mortification of what is sinful, but an abstinence even from God's blessings.

Consider the following declaration of our Savior. He first tells us, "the gate is narrow and the way is hard, that leads to life, and those who find it are few" (Mt 7:14). And again, "Strive to enter by the narrow door; for many, I tell you, will seek to enter and will not be able" (Lk 13:24). Then he explains to us what this peculiar difficulty of a Christian's life consists in: "If any one comes to me and does not hate his own father and mother and wife and children and brothers and sisters, yes, and even his own life, he cannot be my disciple" (Lk 14:26).

Now whatever is precisely meant by this, so far is evident, that our Lord enjoins a certain refraining, not merely from sin, but from innocent comforts and enjoyments of this life, or a self-denial in things lawful.

Again, he says, "If any man would come after me, let him deny himself and take up his cross daily and follow me" (Lk 9:23). Here he shows us from his own example what Christian self-denial is. It is taking on us a cross after his pattern, not a mere refraining from sin, for he had no sin, but a giving up what we might lawfully use. This was the peculiar character in which Christ came on earth. It was this spontaneous and exuberant self-denial which brought him down. He who was one with God took upon him our nature and suffered death, and why? To save us whom he needed not save. Thus he denied himself and took up his cross. This is the very aspect in which God, as revealed in Scripture, is distinguished from that exhibition of his glory which nature gives us. Power, wisdom, love, mercy, long-suffering: these attributes, though far more fully and clearly displayed in Scripture than in nature, still are in their degree seen on the face of the visible creation. But self-denial, if it may be said, this incomprehensible attribute of Divine Providence, is disclosed to us only in Scripture. "God so loved the world that he gave his only-begotten Son" (Jn 3:16). Here is self-denial. And the Son of God so loved us that "though he was rich, yet for your sake he became poor" (2 Cor 8:9). Here is our Savior's self-denial. "Christ did not please himself" (Rom 15:3).

Christian self-denial is incumbent upon us for many reasons. The Christian denies himself in things lawful because he is aware of his own weakness and liability to sin. He dares not walk on the edge of a precipice; instead of going to the extreme of what is allowable, he keeps at a distance from evil, that he may be safe. He abstains lest he should not be temperate. He fasts lest he should eat and drink with the drunken. As is evident, many things are in themselves right and unexceptionable which are inexpedient in the case of a weak and sinful creature. Many kinds of food, good for a man in health, are hurtful when he is ill. Wine is poison to a man in a fierce fever. And just so, many acts, thoughts, and feelings, which would have been allowable in Adam before his fall, are prejudicial or dangerous in man fallen.

Far be it from us, soldiers of Christ, thus to perplex ourselves with this world, who are making our way towards the world to come. "No soldier on service gets entangled in civilian pursuits, since his aim is to satisfy the one who enlisted him. An athlete is not crowned unless he competes according to the rules" (2 Tim 2:4-5). This is St. Paul's rule. Accordingly, in another place, he bears witness to himself that he "died every day" (see 1 Cor 15:31). Day by day he got more and more dead to the world; he had fewer ties to earth, a larger treasure in heaven. Nor let us think that it is over-difficult to imitate him, though we be not apostles, nor are called to any extraordinary work, nor are enriched with any miraculous gifts. He would have all men like himself, and all may be like him, according to their place and measure of grace. If we would be followers of the great apostle, first let us with him fix our eyes upon Christ our Savior, consider the splendor and glory of his holiness, and try to love it. Let us strive and pray that the love of holiness may be created within our hearts, and then acts will follow such as befit us and our circumstances in due time, without our distressing ourselves to find what they should be. You need not attempt to draw any precise line between what is sinful and what is only allowable: look up to Christ and deny yourselves everything, whatever its character, which you think he would have you relinquish. You need not perplex yourselves with points of curiosity if you have a heart to venture after him. True, difficulties will sometimes arise, but they will be seldom. He bids you take up your cross. Therefore, accept the daily opportunities which occur of yielding to others, when you need not yield, and of doing unpleasant services, which you might avoid. He bids those who would be highest, live as the lowest. Therefore, turn from ambitious thoughts and make resolve against taking on you authority and rule. He bids you sell and give alms. Therefore, hate to spend money on yourself. Shut your ears to praise when it grows loud. Set your face like flint when the world ridicules and smile at its threats. Learn to master your heart when it would burst forth into vehemence, or prolong a barren sorrow, or dissolve into unseasonable tenderness. Curb your tongue and turn away your eye lest you fall into temptation. Be up at prayer a great while before day and seek the true Bridegroom. So shall self-denial become natural to you and a change come over you, gently and imperceptibly. And, like Jacob, you will lie down in the waste and will soon see angels and a way opened for you into heaven.

Tuesday of the First Week of Lent

The Power of the Will

The only qualification which will avail us for heaven is the love of God. This changes our whole being. This makes us live. This makes us grow in grace and abound in good works. This makes us fit for God's presence hereafter.

No one can doubt that we are again and again exhorted in Scripture to be holy and perfect, to be holy and blameless in the sight of God, to be holy as he is holy, to keep the commandments, to fulfil the Law, to be filled with the fruit of righteousness. Why do we not obey as we ought? Many people will answer that we have a fallen nature which hinders us; that we cannot help it, though we ought to be very sorry for it. Not so. We can help it. We are not hindered. What we want is the will, and it is our own fault if we have it not. God has abounded in his mercies to us. We have a depth of power and strength lodged in us, but we have not the heart, we have not the will, we have not the love to use it. We lack this one thing: a desire to be new made. And I think anyone who examines himself carefully will own that he does and that this is the reason why he cannot and does not obey or make progress in holiness.

Why is it that we so often wish to do right and cannot? Why is it that we are so frail, feeble, languid, wayward, dim-sighted, fluctuating? Why is it that we cannot "do what [we] want?" (Rom 7:15). Why is it that, day after day, we remain irresolute, that we serve God so poorly, that we govern ourselves so weakly and so variably, that we cannot command our thoughts, that we are so slothful, so cowardly, so discontented, so sensual, so ignorant? Why is it that we, who trust that we are not by willful sin thrown out of grace, who are ruled by no evil masters and bent upon no earthly ends, who are not covetous, or profligate, or worldly-minded, or ambitious, or envious, or proud, or unforgiving, or desirous of name: why is it that we, in the very kingdom of grace, surrounded by angels, and preceded by saints, nevertheless can do so little, and instead of mounting with wings like eagles, grovel in the dust and do but sin and confess sin alternately? Is it that the power of God is not within us? Is it literally that we are not able to perform God's commandments? God forbid! We are able. We have that given us which makes us able. We are not in a state of nature. We have had the gift of grace implanted in us. We have a power within us to do what we are commanded to do. What is it we lack? The power? No. The will. What we lack is the real, simple, earnest, sincere inclination and aim to use what God has given us and what we have in us. Our experience tells us this. It is no matter of mere doctrine, much less a matter of words, but of things: a very plain practical matter.

Hence the great stress laid in Scripture on growing in grace. Seeds are intended to grow into trees. We are regenerated in order that we may be renewed daily after the image of him who has regenerated us. "Be strong in the Lord," says the apostle, "and in the strength of his might" (Eph 6:10). "Put on the whole armor of God" (Eph 6:11), with your loins girt about with truth, the breastplate of righteousness, your feet shod with the preparation of the gospel of peace, the shield of faith, the helmet of salvation, the sword of the Spirit. One grace and then another is to be perfected in us. Each day is to bring forth its own treasure, till we stand, like blessed spirits, able and waiting to do the will of God.

Love can do all things. "Love never ends" (1 Cor 13:8). He that has the will, has the power. If we will, it is doubtless from God, who gave us the power to will. But it is from ourselves too, because we have used that power which God gave. God enables us to will and to do. By nature we cannot will, but by grace we can. And now if we do not will, we are the cause of the defect. What can Almighty Mercy do for us which he has not done? He has "granted to us all things that pertain to life and godliness" (2 Pet 1:3), and we, in consequence, can confirm our "call and election" (2 Pet 1:10) as the holy men of God did of old.

But we sit coldly and sluggishly at home. We fold our hands and cry for "a little slumber" (see Prov 6:10). We shut our eyes, we cannot see things afar off, we cannot see "a land that stretches afar" (Is 33:17). We do not understand that Christ calls us after him. We do not hear the voice of his heralds in the wilderness. We have not the heart to go forth to him who multiplies the loaves and feeds us by every word of his mouth. Other children of Adam have before now done in his strength what we put aside. We fear to be too holy. Others put us to shame. All around us, others are doing what we will not. Others are entering deeper into the kingdom of heaven than we. Others are fighting against their enemies more truly and bravely. The unlettered, the ungifted, the young, the weak and simple, with sling and stones from the brook are encountering Goliath, as having on divine armor. The Church is rising up around us day by day towards heaven, and we do nothing but object, or explain away, or criticize, or make excuses, or wonder. We fear to cast in our lot with the saints. We fear to seek the straight gate. Oh may we be loyal and affectionate before our race is run! Before our sun goes down in the grave, oh may we learn somewhat more of what the apostle calls "the love of Christ which surpasses knowledge" (Eph 3:19) and catch some of the rays of love which come from him! Especially at this season of the year, when Christ calls us into the wilderness, let us gird up our loins and fearlessly obey the summons. Let us take up our cross and follow him. Let us take to us "the whole armor of God, that you may be able to stand against the wiles of the devil. For we are not contending against flesh and blood, but against the principalities, against the powers, against the world rulers of this present darkness, against the spiritual hosts of wickedness in the heavenly places. Therefore take the whole armor of God, that you may be able to withstand in the evil day, and having done all, to stand" (Eph 6:11-13).

Wednesday of the First Week of Lent

The Gospel Sign Addressed to Faith

Although Christ had wrought among them "works which no one else did" (Jn 15:24), and one of their own company had confessed that no man could do miracles such as his "unless God is with him" (Jn 3:2), the scribes and Pharisees persisted in asking for some decisive sign that would prove his divinity beyond all question. In his reply, our Lord denied and yet promised such a sign. He says, "An evil and adulterous generation seeks for a sign; but no sign shall be given to it except the sign of the prophet Jonah" (Mt 12:39). In this sentence it is implied both that their wishes were not to be granted and that a great miracle was to be wrought.

Now what is remarkable in this passage is this, that our Lord promised a great sign parallel to those wrought by the prophets, yet instead of being public as theirs was, it was to be like Jonah's, a secret sign. Few saw it. It was to be received by all, but on faith. It was addressed to the humble and lowly. When it took place, and St. Thomas refused to believe without sight, our Lord said to him, "You have believed because you have seen me. Blessed are those who have not seen and yet believe" (Jn 20:29). The apostle, perhaps, might have been arguing, "If this be the Lord's great sign, surely it is to be seen. What is meant by the resurrection but an evidence which is to be addressed to my senses? I have to believe, and this is to assure my belief." Yet St. Thomas would have been more blessed had he believed Christ's miraculous presence without seeing it, and our Lord implied that such persons there would be.

There was another occasion on which the Jews asked for a sign, and on which our Lord answered by promising one, not to his apostles only, but to all his faithful followers. And it was a sign not more sensible or palpable, not less the object of faith than that sign of his resurrection. He had just before been feeding five thousand men with five barley loaves and two small fishes, when, not contented with this, the Jews said, "what sign do you do, that we may see, and believe you? What work do you perform?" (Jn 6:30). And they proceeded to refer to the sign from heaven which Moses had given them. "Our fathers ate the manna in the wilderness; as it is written, 'He gave them bread from heaven to eat'" (Jn 6:31). It was a little thing, they seemed to say, to multiply bread, but it was a great thing to send down bread from heaven, a great thing, when the nature of the creature was changed, and men were made to live by the word of the Lord. Was the Son of Man able to give them bread such as this?

Yes, surely, he had a sign. It is a sign greater than manna, yet beyond dispute a sign not addressed to sight, but to faith. For our Lord says, "come to me" (Jn 6:65) and "believe in me" (Jn 14:1). And he says, "It is the spirit that gives life, the flesh is of no avail" (Jn 6:63). And he warns us, "No one can come to me unless the Father who sent me draws him" (Jn 6:44). His coming up from the heart of the earth was a sign for faith, not for sight, and such is his coming down from heaven as bread.

What is true in these instances is true of all the parts of our Lord's gracious economy. He was "manifested in the flesh, vindicated in the Spirit, seen by angels, preached among the nations, believed on in the world, taken up in glory" (1 Tim 3:16). Yet what was the nature of the manifestation? The annunciation was secret. The nativity was secret. The miraculous fasting in the wilderness was secret. The resurrection secret. The ascension not far from secret. The abiding presence secret. One thing alone was public and in the eyes of the world: his death. It was the only event which did not speak of his divinity, the only event in which he seemed a sign not of power but of weakness. He was crucified in weakness, but he was not crucified in secret. His humiliation was proclaimed and manifested all over the earth. When lifted up from the earth, he indeed displayed his power: he drew all men to him. But not from what was seen, but from what was hidden—from what was not known, from what was matter of faith, from his atoning virtue. As far as he was seen, he was, in holy Simeon's words, "a sign that is spoken against" (Lk 2:34). It is not by reason or by sight that we accept and glory in the Sign of the Cross. It is by laying aside "all malice and all guile and insincerity and envy and all slander" and like "newborn infants" longing for "the pure spiritual milk" that we may grow thereby (1 Pet 2:1-2).

Let us not seek then for signs and wonders or ask for sensible inward tokens of God's favor. Faith only can introduce us to the unseen presence of God. Let us venture to believe, and the evidence which others demand before believing, we shall gain more abundantly by believing. Almighty God is hidden from us. The world does not discover him to us. We may go to the right hand and to the left, but we find him not. The utmost we can do in the way of nature is to feel after him, who, though we see him not, yet is not far from every one of us.

Once it was not so. Man was created upright, and then he saw his God. He fell and lost God's presence. How must he regain his privilege but by becoming what he once was? He lost it by sinning; he must regain it by purity. And till this recovery, he must accept it on faith. He is allowed to apprehend and enjoy it by faith. He begins with faith, that he may end with holiness. Faith is the religion of sinners beginning to purify themselves for God, and in every age and under every dispensation the just have lived by faith. For we "walk by faith, not by sight" (2 Cor 5:7), and we "look not to the things that are seen but to the things that are unseen" (2 Cor 4:18). We set him on our right hand, him whom "without having seen," we love, and in whom we believe and "rejoice with unutterable and exalted joy." And through this faith we obtain "the salvation of our souls" (see 1 Pet 1:8-9).

Thursday of the First Week of Lent

Profession without Ostentation

Our Savior gives us a command to manifest our religious profession before all men. "You are the light of the world," he says to his disciples: "A city set on a hill cannot be hidden. Nor do men light a lamp and put it under a bushel, but on a stand, and it gives light to all in the house. Let your light so shine before men, that they may see your good works and give glory to your Father who is in heaven" (Mt 5:14-16). Yet presently he says, "when you give alms," "when you pray," "when you fast," do not be "seen by men but by your Father who is in secret" (Mt 6:2-18). How are these commands to be reconciled? How are we at once to profess ourselves Christians and yet hide our Christian words, deeds, and self-denials?

First, much might be said on that mode of witnessing Christ which consists in conforming to his Church. He who simply did what the Church bids would witness a good confession to the world and one which cannot be hid, and at the same time with very little personal display. He does only what he is told to do; he takes no responsibility on himself. Irreligious men will call such a one boastful, or austere, or a hypocrite: that is not the question. The question is whether in God's judgment he deserves the censure, whether he is not as Christ would have him, whether he is not, in thus acting, preaching Christ without hurting his own pureness, gentleness, and modesty of character.

Now, in the next place, consider how great a profession—and yet a profession how unconscious and modest—arises from the mere ordinary manner in which any strict Christian lives. Let this thought be a satisfaction to uneasy minds which fear lest they are not confessing Christ yet dread to display. Your life displays Christ without your intending it. You cannot help it. Your words and deeds will show in the long run where your treasure is and your heart. Out of the abundance of your heart your mouth speaks words "seasoned with salt" (Col 4:6). Wait on God and be doing good and you must, you cannot but be showing your light before men as a city on a hill.

Still it is quite true that there are circumstances under which a Christian is bound openly to express his opinion on religious subjects and matters, and this is the real difficulty: how to do so without display. We must never countenance sin and error. Now the more obvious and modest way of discountenancing evil is by silence and by separating from it. For example, St. Paul expressly tells us "not to associate with any one who bears the name of brother if he is guilty of immorality or greed, or is an idolater, reviler, drunkard, or robber—not even to eat with such a one" (1 Cor 5:11). And St. John gives us like advice with respect to heretics. "If any one comes to you and does not bring this doctrine," (that is, the true doctrine of Christ) "do not receive him into the house or give him any greeting; for he who greets him shares his wicked work" (2 Jn 10-11). It is plain that such conduct on our part requires no great display, for it is but conforming to the rules of the Church, though it is often difficult to know on what occasions we ought to adopt it, which is another question.

A more difficult duty is that of passing judgment (as a Christian is often bound to do) on events of the day and public men. It becomes his duty, in proportion as he has station and influence in the community, in order that he may persuade others to think as he does. This may be done without injury to our Christian gentleness and humbleness, though it is difficult to do it. We need not be angry nor use contentious words, and yet we may frankly give our opinion, in proportion as we have the means of forming one, and be zealous towards God in all active good service.

Another and still more difficult duty is that of personally rebuking those we meet in the intercourse of life who sin in word or deed and testifying before them in Christ's name. That is, it is difficult at once to be unassuming and zealous in such cases. We know it is a plain and repeated precept of Christ to tell others of their faults for charity's sake, but how is this to be done without seeming, nay, without being arrogant and severe? Although to rebuke is a duty, it is not a duty belonging at once to all men, and the perplexity which is felt about it often arises from the very impropriety of attempting it in the particular case. It is improper, as a general rule, in the young to witness before the old otherwise than by their silence. Still more improper is it in inferiors to rebuke their superiors, for instance, a child his parent or a private person his divinely-appointed governor. When we assume a character not suited to us, of course we feel awkward, and although we may have done so in honesty and zeal (however ill-tutored) and so God may in mercy accept our service, still he rebukes us by our very feeling of perplexity and shame.

It is to be considered, too, that to do the part of witness for the truth, to warn and rebuke, is not an elementary duty of a Christian. Our duties come in a certain order, some before others, and this is not one of the first of them. Our first duties are to repent and believe. It would be strange indeed for a man who had just begun to think of religion to set up for some great one, to assume he was a saint and a witness and to exhort others to turn to God. This is evident. But as time goes on and his religious character becomes formed, then, while he goes on to perfection in all his duties, he takes upon himself, in the number of these, to witness for God by word of mouth. It is difficult to say when a man has leave openly to rebuke others: certainly not before he has considerable humility.

Friday of the First Week of Lent

God's Commandments Not Burdensome

It must ever be borne in mind that it is a very great and arduous thing to attain to heaven. "Many are called, but few are chosen" (Mt 22:14). "The gate is narrow and the way is hard" (Mt 7:14). "Many, I tell you, will seek to enter and will not be able" (Lk 13:24). "If any one comes to me and does not hate his own father and mother and wife and children and brothers and sisters, yes, and even his own life, he cannot be my disciple" (Lk 14:26). On the other hand, it is evident to anyone who reads the New Testament with attention that Christ and his apostles speak of a religious life as something easy, pleasant, and comfortable. "This is the love of God, that we keep his commandments. And his commandments are not burdensome" (1 Jn 5:3). In like manner, our Savior says, "Come to me . . . I will give you rest. . . . my yoke is easy, and my burden is light" (Mt 11:28-30).

How is it that these apparently opposite declarations of Christ and his apostles are fulfilled to us? It is obvious that obedience to God's commandments is ever easy and almost without effort to those who begin to serve him from the beginning of their days, whereas those who wait a while find it burdensome in proportion to their delay.

Thus Christ's commandments, viewed as he enjoins them on us, are not burdensome. They would be burdensome if put upon us all at once. But they are not heaped on us according to his order of dispensing them, which goes upon an harmonious

49

and considerate plan: by little and little, first one duty, then another, then both, and so on. Moreover, they come upon us while the safeguard of virtuous principle is forming naturally and gradually in our minds by our very deeds of obedience and is following them as their reward. Now, if men will not take their duties in Christ's order, but are determined to delay obedience with the intention of setting about their duty some day or other and then making up for past time, is it wonderful that they find it burdensome and difficult to perform? That they are overwhelmed with the arrears of their great work, that they are entangled and stumble amid the intricacies of the Divine system which has progressively enlarged upon them?

These thoughts tend to humble every one of us. For, however faithfully we have obeyed God, and however early we began to do so, surely we might have begun sooner than we did and might have served him more heartily. We cannot but be conscious of this. Individuals among us may be more or less guilty, as the case may be, but the best and worst among us may well unite themselves together so far as this, to confess that they erred and strayed from God's ways like lost sheep and have followed too much the devices and desires of their own hearts. Some of us may be nearer Heaven, some further from it. Some may have a good hope of salvation, and others (God forbid! but it may be) no present hope. Still let us unite now as one body in confessing ourselves sinners, deserving God's anger, and having no hope except according to his promises declared unto mankind in Christ Jesus our Lord. He who first regenerated us and then gave his commandments, and then was so ungratefully deserted by us, he again it is that must pardon and quicken us after our accumulated guilt, if we are to be pardoned. Let us then trace back in memory our early years—what we were when five years old, when ten, when fifteen, when twenty—what our state would have been as far as we can guess it had God taken us to our account at any age before the present.

Let each of us reflect upon his own most gross and persevering neglect of God at various seasons of his past life. How considerate he has been to us! How did he shield us from temptation! How did he open his will gradually upon us, as we might be able to bear it! How has he done all things well, so that the spiritual work might go on calmly, safely, surely! How did he lead us on, duty by duty, as if step by step upwards, by the easy rounds of that ladder whose top reaches to Heaven? Yet how did we thrust ourselves into temptation! How did we refuse to come to him that we might have life! How did we daringly sin against light! And what was the consequence? That our work grew beyond our strength, or rather that our strength grew less as our duties increased, till at length we gave up obedience in despair. And yet then he still tarried and was merciful unto us. He turned and looked upon us to bring us into repentance, and for a while we were moved. Yet even then our wayward hearts could not keep up to their own resolves, letting go again the heat which Christ gave them, as if made of stone and not of living flesh. What could have been done more to his vineyard that he has not done in it? "O my people, what have I done to you? In what have I wearied you? Answer me! For I brought you up from the land of Egypt, and redeemed you from the house of bondage" (Mic 6:3-4). He has showed us what is good, and he shed his Holy Spirit on us that we might love him. "And this is the love of God, that we keep his commandments. And his commandments are not burdensome" (1 Jn 5:3). Why, then, have they been burdensome to us? Why have we erred from his ways and hardened our hearts from his fear? Why do we this day stand ashamed, yes, even confounded, because we bear the reproach of our youth?

Let us then turn to the Lord while yet we may. Difficult it will be in proportion to the distance we have departed from him. Since every one might have done more than he has done, every one has suffered losses he never can make up. We have made his commands burdensome to us: we must bear it. Let us not attempt to explain them away because they are burdensome. We never can wash out the stains of sin. God may forgive, but the sin has had its work and its memento is set up in the soul. God sees it there. Earnest obedience and prayer will gradually remove it. Still, what miserable loss of time is it, in our brief life, to be merely undoing (as has become necessary) the evil which we have done, instead of going on to perfection! If by God's grace we shall be able in a measure to sanctify ourselves in spite of our former sins, yet how much more should we have attained, had we always been engaged in his service.

These are bitter and humbling thoughts, but they are good thoughts if they lead us to repentance.

Saturday of the First Week of Lent

Contracted Views in Religion

"Behold, these many years I have served you, and I never disobeyed your command; yet you never gave me a kid, that I might make merry with my friends" (Lk 15:29). The elder brother of the prodigal complained of his father's kindness towards the penitent, in perplexity and distress of mind. Accordingly, he was comforted by his father, who graciously informed him of the reason of his acting as he had done. "Son, you are always with me," he says, "and all that is mine is yours. It was fitting to make merry and be glad, for this your brother was dead, and is alive; he was lost, and is found" (Lk 15:31-32).

Let us try to understand the feelings of the elder brother and to apply the picture to the circumstances in which we find ourselves.

In the conduct of the father, there seemed at first sight an evident departure from the rules of fairness and justice. Here was a reprobate son received into his favor on the first stirrings of repentance. What was the use of serving him dutifully if there were no difference in the end between the righteous and the wicked? This is what we feel and act upon in life constantly. In doing good to the poor, for instance, a chief object is to encourage industrious and provident habits; and it is evident we should hurt and disappoint the better sort, and defeat our object, if we did not take into account the difference of their conduct, though we promised to do so, but gave those who did not work all the benefits granted to those who did. The elder brother's case, then, seemed a hard one; and that, even without supposing him to feel jealous or to have unsuitable notions of his own importance and usefulness. Apply this to the case of religion, and it still holds good. At first sight, the reception of the penitent sinner seems to interfere with the reward of the faithful servant of God. Just as the promise of pardon is abused by bad men to encourage themselves in sinning on, so it is misapprehended by the good so as to dispirit them. For what is our great stay and consolation amid the perturbations of this world? The truth and justice of God, our one light in the midst of darkness.

Now the restoration of sinners seems, at first sight, to put bad and good on a level. And the feeling it excites in the mind is expressed in the parable by the words of the elder son: "these many years I have served you, and I never disobeyed your command," yet I never have been welcomed and honored with that peculiar joy which you show towards the repentant sinner. This is the expression of an agitated mind, that fears lest it be cast back upon the wide world to grope in the dark without a God to guide and encourage it in its course.

The condescending answer of the father in the parable is most instructive. It sanctions the great truth, which seemed in jeopardy, that it is not the same thing in the end to obey or disobey, expressly telling us that the Christian penitent is not placed on a footing with those who have consistently served God from the first. "Son, you are always with me, and all that is mine is yours." That is, why this sudden fear and distrust? Can there be any misconception on your part because I welcome your brother? Do you not yet understand me? Surely you have known me too long to suppose that you can lose by his gain. You are in my confidence. I do not make any outward display of kindness towards you, for it is a thing to be taken for granted. We give praise and make professions to strangers, not to friends. You are my heir, all that I have is yours. "O you of little faith, why did you doubt?" (Mt 14:31). Who could have thought that it were needful to tell you truths which you have heard all your life?

Let us now notice the unworthy feeling which appears in the conduct of the elder brother. "He was angry" and would not go into the house (Lk 15:28). How may this be fulfilled in our own case? Good men are, like Elijah, "jealous for the Lord, the God of hosts" (1 Kings 19:10), and rightly solicitous to see his tokens around them, the pledges of his unchangeable just government, but then they mix with such good feelings undue notions of self-importance of which they are not aware. This seemingly was the state of mind which dictated the complaint of the elder brother.

The elder brother had always lived at home. He had seen things go on one way, and, as was natural and right, got attached to them in that one way. He thought he understood his father's ways and principles far more than he did, and when an occurrence took place for which he had hitherto met with no precedent, he lost himself, as being suddenly thrust aside out of the contracted circle in which he had hitherto walked. He was disconcerted and angry with his father. And so in religion, we have need to watch against that narrowness of mind to which we are tempted by the uniformity and tranquility of God's providence towards us. We should be on our guard lest we suppose ourselves to have such a clear knowledge of God's ways as to rely implicitly on our own notions and feelings.

Something of the character of the elder brother may perchance be found among ourselves. We have long had the inestimable blessings of peace and quiet. We are unworthy of the least of God's mercies, much more of the greatest. But with the blessings we have the trial. Let us then guard against abusing our happy lot, while we have it, or we may lose it for having abused it. Let us guard against discontent in any shape, and as we cannot help hearing what goes on in the world, let us guard, on hearing it, against all intemperate, uncharitable feelings towards those who differ with us or oppose us. Let us pray for our enemies. Let us try to make out men to be as good as they can fairly and safely be considered. Let us rejoice at any symptoms of repentance or any marks of good principle in those who are on the side of error. Let us be forgiving. Let us try to be very humble, to understand our ignorance, and to rely constantly on the enlightening grace of our Great Teacher. Let us be slow to speak, slow to wrath, not abandoning our principles, or shrinking from the avowal of them when seasonable, or going over to the cause of error, or fearing consequences, but acting ever from a sense of duty, not from passion, pride, jealousy, or an unbelieving dread of the future. "Son, you are always with me, and all that is mine is yours." What a gracious announcement, if we could realize it! And how consoling, so far as we have reason to hope that we are following on to know God's will and living in his faith and fear. What should alarm those who have Christ's power or make them envious who have Christ's fullness? We ought calmly to regard and resolutely to endure the petty workings of an evil world, thinking seriously of nothing but of the souls that are perishing in it.

Second Sunday in Lent

The World and Sin

Our Lord often passed the night in prayer, and, as afterwards in that sad night before his passion, he took with him three apostles to witness his prayer in agony, so at an earlier time he took the same favored three with him to witness his prayer in ecstasy and glory. On the one occasion, he fell on his face and prayed more earnestly till he was covered with a sweat of blood which rolled down upon the cold earth. In the other, as he prayed his countenance became bright and glorious, and he was lifted off the earth. So he remained communing with his Father, ministered to by Moses and Elijah, till a voice came from the cloud, which said, "This is my Son, my Chosen; listen to him!" (Lk 9:35). The sight had been so wonderful, so transporting, that St. Peter could not help crying out, "Master, it is well that we are here" (Lk 9:33). Simple words, but how much they contain in them. His reason did not speak, but his affections. He did but say that it was good to be there. And he wished that great good to continue.

Now let us see what was taking place below. When they reached the crowd, they found a dispute going on between the rest of the apostles and the scribes. A father had brought his son to be cured by the apostles. He was a frightful maniac, possessed by the devil. He sometimes dashed himself to the ground, threw himself into the fire or into the water, foamed at the mouth, and then collapsed. The devil was too much for the apostles. They could not cast him out. They were reduced to a sort of despair, and this was the occasion of their dispute with the scribes, who might be taunting them with their failure. Oh, the contrast between what St. Peter had come from, and what he had now come to! He had left peace, stillness, contemplation, the vision of heaven, and he had come into pain, grief, confusion, perplexity, disappointment, and debate.

Now this contrast between the Mount of Transfiguration and the scene at its foot fitly represents to us the contrast between the world and the Church, between the things seen and the things unseen.

The poor youth who was brought to Christ was possessed by the devil, and alas! is not a great portion, is not the greatest portion of mankind at this day possessed by the devil too? He is called in Scripture "the god of this world" (2 Cor 4:4), and "the prince of the power of the air, the spirit that is now at work in the sons of disobedience" (Eph 2:2). He is found all over the earth, and within the souls of men, not indeed able to do anything which God does not permit, but still, God not interfering, he possesses immense power. And as the poor epileptic in the gospel was under the mastery of the evil spirit, so that his eyes, his ears, his tongue, his limbs were not his own, so does that same miserable spirit possess the souls of sinners, ruling them, impelling them here and there, doing what he will with them; some he moves one way, some in another, but all in some pitiable, horrible, and ungodly way.

Wickedness is sometimes called madness in Scripture. As literal madness is derangement of the reason, so sin is derangement of the heart, of the spirit, of the affection. And as madness was the disorder in which possession by the devil showed itself in Scripture, so this madness of the heart and spirit is the disorder which in all ages the devil produces in the spirit. And as there are different forms of that madness which is derangement of the reason, so there are different forms of that worse madness which is sin.

When St. Peter, St. James, and St. John came down from the Mount and saw the miserable youth tormented by an evil spirit, they saw in that youth a figure and emblem of that world of sinners, to whom in due time they were to be sent to preach. But this is not all. They found their brethren disputing with the scribes, or at least the scribes questioning with them. Here is another circumstance in which the scene which they saw resembled the world. The world is full of wrangling and debate because when the heart is wrong, the reason goes wrong too, and when men corrupt themselves and lead bad lives, then they do not see the truth, and this creates a great confusion. The evil spirit has blinded the eyes of them that do not believe, and hence they are obliged to wrangle and debate, for they have lost their way; and they fall out with each other and one says this and one says that, because they do not see.

There is an immense weight of evil in the world. We Catholics have it in charge to resist, to overcome the evil; but we cannot do what we would, we cannot overcome the giant, we cannot bind the strong man. We do a part of the work, not all. It is a battle which goes on between good and evil, and though by God's grace we do something, we cannot do more. There is confusion of nations and perplexity. It is God's will that so it should be, to show his power. He alone can heal the soul. He alone can expel the devil. And therefore, we must wait for a great deal, till he comes down from his seat on high, his seat in glory, to aid us and deliver us.

In that day we shall enter, if we be worthy, the fullness of that glory, of which the three apostles had the foretaste in the moment of Transfiguration. All is darkness here, all is bright in heaven. All is disorder here, all is order there. Here we are in a state of uncertainty. The Church suffers; her goodly portion, and her choice inheritance suffer; the vineyard is laid waste; there is persecution and war, and Satan rages and afflicts when he cannot destroy. But all this will be set right in the world to come. For then we shall be like our Lord himself, we shall have glorified bodies, as he had then and has now. We shall have put off flesh and blood, and receive our bodies at the last day, the same indeed, but incorruptible, spiritual bodies, which will be able to see and enjoy the presence of God in a way which was beyond the three apostles in the days of their mortality. Then the envious malignant spirit will be cast out, and we shall have nothing to fear, nothing to be perplexed at, for the Lord God shall lighten us, and encompass us, and we shall be in perfect security and peace. Then we shall look back upon this world, and the trials and temptations which are past, and what thankfulness will rise within us; and we shall look forward, and this one thought will be upon us that this blessedness is to last forever. It is not that we shall be promised a hundred years of peace, or a thousand, but for ever and ever shall we be as we are, for our happiness and our peace will be founded in the infinite blessedness and peace of God, and as he is eternal and happy, so shall we be.

Monday of the Second Week of Lent

The Invisible World

We think that we are lords of the world who may do as we will. We think the earth our property, and its movements in our power, whereas it has higher lords besides us and is the scene of a higher conflict than we are capable of conceiving. It contains Christ's little ones and his angels, and these at length shall take possession of it and be manifested. At present, all things, to appearance, continue as they were from the beginning of the creation, and scoffers ask, "Where is the promise of his coming?" But at the appointed time there will be a "revealing of the sons of God" (Rom 8:19), and the hidden saints "will shine like the sun in the kingdom of their Father" (Mt 13:43). When the angels appeared to the shepherds it was a sudden appearance: "suddenly there was with the angel a multitude of the heavenly host" (Lk 2:13). How wonderful a sight! The night had before seemed just like any other night, as the evening on which Jacob saw the vision seemed like any other evening. They were keeping watch over their sheep; they were watching the night as it passed. The stars moved on. It was midnight. They had no idea of such a thing when the angel appeared. Such are the power and virtue hidden in things which are seen, and at God's will they are manifested. They were manifested for a moment to Jacob, for a moment to Elisha's servant, for a moment to the shepherds. They will be manifested for ever when Christ comes at the Last Day in "the glory of the Father and of the holy angels" (Lk 9:26). Then this world will fade away and the other world will shine forth.

Let these be our thoughts in the spring season, when the whole face of nature is so rich and beautiful. Once only in the year does the world which we see show forth its hidden powers and in a manner manifest itself. Then the leaves come out, and the grass and the corn spring up. There is a sudden rush and burst outwardly of that hidden life which God has lodged in the material world. It shows us what it can do at God's command, when he gives the word. This earth, which now buds forth in leaves and blossoms, will one day burst forth into a new world of light and glory, in which we shall see saints and angels dwelling. Who would think, except from his experience of former springs all through his life, who could conceive two or three months before that it was possible that the face of nature, which then seemed so lifeless, should become so splendid and varied? The season may delay but come it will at last. So it is with the coming of that Eternal Spring for which all Christians are waiting. Yet though it tarry, let us wait for it, for "it will surely come, it will not delay" (Hab 2:3). Therefore we say day by day, "Thy Kingdom come," which means, "O Lord, show yourself, manifest yourself, stir up your strength and come and help us." The earth that we see does not satisfy us. It is but a beginning. It is but a promise of something beyond it. Even with all its blossoms on, yet it is not enough. We know much more lies hid in it than we see. A world of saints and angels, a glorious world, the palace of God, the mountain of the Lord of Hosts, the heavenly Jerusalem, the throne of God and Christ: all these wonders, everlasting, all-precious, mysterious, and incomprehensible, lie hid in what we see. What we see is the outward shell of an eternal kingdom, and on that kingdom we fix the eyes of our faith. Shine forth, O Lord, as when on your Nativity your angels visited the shepherds. Let your glory blossom forth as bloom and foliage on the trees. Change with your mighty power this visible world into that diviner world, which as yet we see not. Destroy what we see, that it may pass and be transformed into what we believe. Bright as is the sun, and the sky, and the clouds, green as are the leaves and the fields, sweet as is the singing of the birds, we know that they are not all, and we will not take up with a part for the whole. They proceed from a center of love of goodness which is God himself, but they are not his fullness. They speak of heaven, but they are not heaven. They are but as stray beams and dim reflections of his image. We are looking for the coming of the day of God, when all this outwards world, fair though it be, shall perish, when the heavens shall be burnt, and the earth melt away. We know that to remove the world which is seen will be the manifestation of the world which is not seen. We know that what we see is as a screen hiding from us God and Christ and his saints and angels. And we earnestly desire and pray for the dissolution of all that we see from our longing after that which we do not see.

Blessed are they who shall at length behold what as yet mortal eye has not seen and faith only enjoys! Those wonderful things of the new world are even now as they shall be then. They are immortal and eternal, and the souls who shall then be made conscious of them will see them in their calmness and their majesty where they ever have been. But who can express the surprise and rapture which will come upon those who then at last apprehend them for the first time and to whose perceptions they are new! Who can imagine by a stretch of fancy the feelings of those who having died in faith wake up to enjoyment! The life then begun, we know, will last forever. Yet surely if memory be to us then what it is now, that will be a day much to be observed unto the Lord through all ages of eternity. We may increase indeed forever in knowledge and in love, still that first waking from the dead, the day at once of our birth and our espousals, will be ever endeared and hallowed in our thoughts. When we find ourselves after long rest gifted with fresh powers, vigorous with the seed of eternal life with us, able to love God as we wish, conscious that all trouble, sorrow, pain, anxiety, bereavement is over forever, blessed in the full affection of those earthly friends whom we loved so poorly and could protect so feebly while they were with us in the flesh, and, above all, visited by the immediate visible ineffable presence of God Almighty, with his only-begotten Son our Lord Jesus Christ, and his co-equal, co-eternal Spirit, that great sight in which is the fullness of joy and pleasure for evermore—what deep, incommunicable, unimaginable thoughts will be then upon us! Earthly words are indeed all worthless to minister to such high anticipations. Let us close our eyes and keep silence.

Tuesday of the Second Week of Lent

The Vanity of Human Glory

In heathen times, when men understood that they had souls, yet did not know what was the soul's true happiness or how it was to be gained, much was thought, and more talked, of what they called glory. Now what exactly they wished to signify by the word "glory" is difficult to say, for they were apt to speak of it as if it were some real thing, and that, too, which one could possess and make one's own. Yet, if we come to consider its real meaning, it plainly stands for nothing else than the praise of other men, the being admired, honored, and feared. Or, more commonly, having a celebrated name, that is, for a something external to ourselves. But whatever precise notions they wished to attach to the word, they used to talk in glowing language of the necessity of going through dangers and suffering for glory's sake, laboring to benefit the world for glory, and dying for glory.

When we read of poor heathens using this language, it is our duty to pity them, for it is plain enough to any sober reasoner that nothing is so vain as to talk of this glory being a real and substantial good. But it is a most melancholy fact that Christians are chargeable with the same foolish irrational sin. It is not wonderful that we should seek the praise of persons we know. We all naturally love to be respected and admired, and in due limits perhaps we may be allowed to do so. The love of praise is capable of receiving a religious discipline and character. But the surprising thing is that we should leave the thought of present goods, without going on to seek the good of the next world. That we should deny ourselves, yet not deny ourselves for a reality but for a shadow. It is natural to love to have deference and respect paid us by our acquaintance, but the praise of a vast multitude of persons we never saw or shall see or care about: this is a depraved appetite, as unmeaning as it is sinful. It is excusable in heathens, who had no better good clearly proposed to them, but in Christians, who have the favor of God and eternal life set before them, it is deeply criminal, for it is a turning away from the bread of heaven to feed upon ashes.

This love of indiscriminate praise is an odious, superfluous, wanton sin, and we should put it away with a manly hatred as something irrational and degrading. Shall man, born for high ends, the servant and son of God, the redeemed of Christ, the heir of immortality, go out of his way to have his mere name praised by a vast populace, or by various people, of whom he knows nothing and most of whom (if he saw them) he would himself be the first to condemn? It is odious, yet young persons of high minds and vigorous powers are especially liable to be led captive by this snare of the devil. If reasoning does not convince them, let facts: the love of glory has its peculiar condemnation in its consequences. No sin has been so productive of widespread enduring ruin among mankind. Wars and conquests are the means by which men have most reckoned on securing it. A tree is known by its fruit.

These remarks apply to the love of indiscriminate praise in all its shapes. Few persons, indeed, are in a condition to be tempted by the love of glory, but all persons may be tempted to indulge in vanity, which is nothing else but the love of general admiration. A vain person is one who likes to be praised, whoever is the praiser, whether good or bad. Now consider, how few men are not in their measure vain till they reach that period of life when by the course of nature vanity disappears?

Let all Christians carefully ask themselves whether they are not very fond, not merely of the praise of their superiors and friends—that is right—but of that of any person, any chance-comer, about whom they know nothing. Who is not open to flattery? And if he seems not to be exposed to it, is it not that he is too shrewd or too refined to be beguiled by any but what is delicate and unostentatious? A man never considers who it is who praises him. But the most dangerous, perhaps, of all kinds of vanity is to be vain of our personal appearance. Such persons are ever under temptation; wherever they go they carry their snare with them. And their idle love of admiration is gratified without effort by the very looks of those who gaze upon them.

Not only must we desire the praise of none but good men, but we must not earnestly desire to be known even by many good men. The truth is, we cannot know, really know, many persons at all, and it is always dangerous to delight in the praises of strangers, even though we believe them to be good men, and much more to seek their praises, which is a kind of ambition. And further to this, it is more agreeable to the Christian temper to be satisfied rather to know and to be known by a few, and to grow day by day in their esteem and affection, than to desire one's name to be on the lips of many, though they profess religion and associate with religious objects. And it is our great privilege to have the real blessing in our power, while the fancied good alone is difficult to be gained. Few Christians can be great or can leave a name to posterity, but most Christians will, in the length of their lives, be able to secure the love and praise of one or two who are to them the representatives of him whom "without having seen . . . [they] love" (1 Pet 1:8), and in whose presence, or at least in whose memory, they may comfort their heart until he comes.

Let us seek this praise which comes of God. Let us seek it, for it is to be obtained; it is given to those worthy of it. The poorest, the oldest, and the most infirm among us, those who are living not merely in obscurity, but are despised and forgotten, who seem to answer no good purpose by living on, and whose death will not be felt even by their neighbors as a loss, these even may obtain our Savior's approving look, and receive the future greeting, "Well done, good and faithful servant" (Mt 25:21).

Wednesday of the Second Week of Lent

Jeremiah, a Lesson for the Disappointed

The prophets were ever ungratefully treated by the Israelites. They were resisted, their warnings neglected, their good services forgotten. But of all the persecuted prophets, Jeremiah is the most eminent, that is, we know more of his history, of his imprisonments, his wanderings, and his afflictions. He may be taken as a representative of the prophets, and hence it is that he is a special type of our Lord and Savior. All the prophets were types of the great prophet whose way they were preparing. They tended towards and spoke of Christ. In their sufferings they foreshadowed his priesthood, and in their miracles his royal power. The history of Jeremiah, as being drawn out in Scripture more circumstantially than that of the other prophets, is the most exact type of Christ among them, that is, next to David, who, of course, was the nearest resemblance to him of all, as a sufferer, an inspired teacher, and a king. Jeremiah comes next to David, not in dignity and privilege, for it was Elijah who was taken up to heaven and appeared at the Transfiguration, nor in inspiration, for to Isaiah one should assign the higher evangelical gifts, but in typifying him who came and wept over Jerusalem and then was tortured and put to death by those he wept over. And hence, when our Lord came, while some thought him Elijah, and others John the Baptist, risen from the dead, there were others who thought him Jeremiah.

Jeremiah's ministry may be summed up in three words: hope, labor, disappointment. It was his privilege to be called to his sacred office from his earliest years. Like Samuel, he was of the tribe of Levi, dedicated from his birth to religious services and favored with the constant presence and grace of God. "Before I formed you in the womb I knew you," says the Word of the Lord to him when he gave him his commission, "and before you were born I consecrated you; I appointed you a prophet to the nations" (Jer 1:5). No prophet commenced his labors with greater encouragement than Jeremiah. A king had succeeded to the throne who was bringing back the times of the man after God's own heart. There had not been a son of David so zealous as Josiah since David himself. The king, too, was young, at most twenty years of age. What might not be effected in a course of years, however corrupt and degraded was the existing state of his people? So Jeremiah might think. Whether or not, however, such hope of success encouraged Jeremiah's first exertions, very soon this cheerful prospect was overcast, and he was left to labor in the dark. He was soon undeceived as to any hopes he might entertain, whether, by the express Word of God informing him, or by the actual hardened state of sin in which the nation lay. Soon were his hopes destroyed and his mind sobered into a more blessed and noble temper: resignation.

Resignation is a more blessed frame of mind than sanguine hope of present success because it is the truer and the more consistent with our fallen state of being and the more improving to our hearts, and because it is that for which the most eminent servants of God have been conspicuous. To expect great effects from our exertions for religious objects is natural and innocent, but it arises from inexperience of the kind of work we have to do: to change the heart and will of man. It is a far nobler frame of mind to labor, not with the hope of seeing the fruit of our labor, but for conscience's sake as a matter of duty. And again, in faith, trusting that good will be done though we see it not. Look through the Bible, and you will find God's servants, even though they began with success, end with disappointment. Not that God's purposes or his instruments fail, but that the time for reaping what we have sown is hereafter, not here. There is no great visible fruit in any one man's lifetime.

In the instance of Jeremiah, we have on record that variety and vicissitude of feelings which this transition from hope to disappointment produces in a sensitive mind. His trials were very great, even in Josiah's reign, but when that pious king's countenance was withdrawn by his early death, he was exposed to persecution from every class of men. At one time, we read of the people conspiring against him, at another, that the men of his own city seek his life on account of his prophesying in the Lord's name (see Jer 11:21). At another time, he was seized by the priests and the prophets in order to be put to death, from which he was only saved by certain of the princes and elders who were still faithful to the memory of Josiah. At another time, King Zedekiah put him in prison. Afterwards, when the army of the Chaldeans had besieged Jerusalem, the Jews accused him of falling away to the enemy and cast him into a dungeon where he "sank in the mire" and almost perished from hunger (Jer 38:6). When Jerusalem had been taken by the enemy, Jeremiah was forcibly carried down to Egypt by men who at first pretended to reverence and consult him, and there he came to his end, it is believed a violent end.

Such were his trials: his affliction, fear, despondency, and sometimes even restlessness under them are variously expressed, the succession and tide of feelings which most persons undergo before their minds settle into the calm of resignation. At length, he is able to express a chastened spirit and weaned heart which is the termination of all agitation and anxiety in the case of religious minds. He, who at one time could not comfort himself, at another was sent to comfort a brother, and, in comforting Baruch, he speaks in that nobler temper of resignation which takes the place of sanguine hope and harassing fear, and betokens calm and clear-sighted faith and inward peace. "Thus says the Lord, the God of Israel, to you, O Baruch. You said, 'Woe is me! for the Lord has added sorrow to my pain; I am weary with my groaning, and I find no rest.' . . . Behold, what I have built I am breaking down, and what I have planted I am plucking up—that is, the whole land. And do you seek great things for yourself? Seek them not; for behold, I am bringing evil upon all flesh . . . but I will give you your life as a prize of war in all places to which you may go" (Jer 45:2-5). That is, seek not success, be not impatient or anxious, and be content if, after all your labors, you do but save yourself without seeing other fruit of them.

Thursday of the Second Week of Lent

The Danger of Riches

Unless we were accustomed to read the New Testament from our childhood, we should be very much struck with the warnings which it contains, not only against the love of riches but the very possession of them. We should wonder with a portion of that astonishment which the apostles at first felt, who had been brought up in the notion that riches were a chief reward which God bestowed on those he loved. As it is, we have heard the most solemn declarations so continually that we have ceased to attach any distinct meaning to them. Or, if our attention is at any time drawn more closely to them, we soon dismiss the subject on some vague imagination that what is said in Scripture had a reference to the particular times when Christ came, without attempting to settle its exact application to us, or whether it has any such application at all.

But even if we had ever so little concern in the Scripture denunciations against riches and the love of riches, their very awfulness might have seemed enough to save them from neglect. And this consideration may lead a man to suspect that the neglect in question does not entirely arise from unconcern, but from a sort of misgiving that the subject of riches is one which cannot be safely or comfortably discussed by the Christian world at this day.

But, in truth, that our Lord meant to speak of riches as being in some sense a calamity to the Christian is plain from his praises and recommendations of poverty. "Sell your possessions, and give alms; provide yourselves with purses that do not grow old" (Lk 12:33). "If you would be perfect, go, sell what you possess and give to the poor, and you will have treasure in heaven" (Mt 19:21). And, "Blessed are you poor, for yours is the kingdom of God" (Lk 6:20). Whatever be the line of conduct these texts prescribe to this or that individual, so far seems clear, that according to the rule of the Gospel, the absence of wealth is, as such, a more blessed and a more Christian state than the possession of it.

The most obvious danger which worldly possessions present to our spiritual welfare is that they become practically a substitute in our hearts for that one object to which our supreme devotion is due. They are present; God is unseen. They are means at hand of effecting what we want; whether God will hear our petitions for those wants is uncertain. Thus they minister to the corrupt inclinations of our nature. They promise and are able to be gods to us, and such gods too as require no service, but, like dumb idols, exalt the worshipper, impressing him with a notion of his own power and security. And in this consist their chief and most subtle mischief. Religious men are able to repress, nay extirpate sinful desires, the lust of the flesh and of the eyes, gluttony, drunkenness, and the like, love of amusements and frivolous pleasures and display, indulgence in luxuries of whatever kind; but as to wealth, they cannot easily rid themselves of a secret feeling that it gives them a footing to stand upon, an importance, a superiority, and in consequence, they get attached to this world, lose sight of the duty of bearing the Cross, become dull and dim-sighted, and lose their delicacy and precision of touch as regards religious interests. To risk all upon Christ's word seems somehow unnatural to them, extravagant, and evidences a morbid excitement. And death, instead of being a gracious release is not a welcome subject of thought. They are content to remain as they are and do not contemplate a change. They desire and mean to serve God, and actually do serve him in their measure, but not with the keen sensibilities, the noble enthusiasm, the grandeur and elevation of soul, the dutifulness and affectionateness towards Christ which become a Christian.

As the danger of possessing riches is the carnal security to which they lead, that of desiring and pursuing them is that an object of this world is thus set before us as the aim and end of life. It seems to be the will of Christ that his followers should have no aim or end, pursuit or business, merely of this world. It is his will that all we do should be done, not unto men, or to the world, or to self, but to his glory, and the more we are enabled to do this simply, the more favored we are. Whenever we act with reference to an object of this world, even though it be ever so pure, we are exposed to the temptation of setting our hearts upon obtaining it, and it is a part of Christian caution to see that our engagements do not become pursuits. Engagements are our portion, but pursuits are for the most part of our own choosing. We may be engaged in worldly business without pursuing worldly objects.

The pursuit of gain, whether in a large or small way, is prejudicial to our spiritual interests in that it fixes the mind upon an object of this world. Money is a sort of creation and gives the acquirer—even more than the possessor—an imagination of his own power and tends to make him idolize self. Again, what we have won at great cost we are unwilling to part with, so that the man who has himself made his wealth will commonly be stingy, or at least will not part with it except in exchange for what will reflect credit upon himself or increase his importance. Even when his conduct is most disinterested and amiable, still this indulgence of self, of pride and worldliness, inserts itself.

Very unlikely therefore is it that he should be liberal towards God, for religious offerings are an expenditure without sensible return, and that upon objects for which the very pursuit of wealth has indisposed his mind.

It is a fearful consideration that we belong to a nation which in good measure subsists by making money. Let us consider that fact in light of our Savior's declarations against wealth and trust in wealth: we shall have abundant matter for serious thought.

Friday of the Second Week of Lent

Self-Denial the Test of Religious Earnestness

The nature of Christian obedience is the same in every age and brings with it an evidence of God's favor. We cannot make ourselves as sure of our being in the number of God's true servants as the early Christians were, yet we may possess our degree of certainty, and by the same kind of evidence, the evidence of self-denial. This was the great evidence which the first disciples gave, and which we can still give. Reflect upon our Savior's plain declarations. "If any man would come after me, let him deny himself and take up his cross and follow me" (Mk 8:34). "If any one comes to me and does not hate his own father and mother and wife and children and brothers and sisters, yes, and even his own life, he cannot be my disciple. Whoever does not bear his own cross and come after me, cannot be my disciple" (Lk 14:26-27). "If your hand causes you to sin, cut it off . . . if your foot causes you to sin, cut it off . . . if your eye causes you to sin, pluck it out; it is better for you to enter into life maimed . . . lame . . . with one eye than . . . to be thrown into hell" (Mk 9:43-47).

From such passages we learn that a rigorous self-denial is a chief duty, nay, that it may be considered the test whether we are Christ's disciples, whether we are living in a mere dream, which we mistake for Christian faith and obedience, or are really and truly awake, alive, living in the day, on our road heavenwards. The early Christians went through self-denials in their very profession of the Gospel. What are our self-denials, now that the profession of the Gospel is not a self-denial? In what sense do we fulfil the words of Christ? Have we any distinct notion what is meant by the words "taking up our cross"? In what way are we acting in which we should not act, supposing the Bible and the Church were unknown to this country, and religion, as existing among us, was merely a fashion of this world? What are we doing which we have reason to trust is done for Christ's sake who bought us?

Works are said to be the fruits and evidence of faith. That faith is said to be dead which has them not. Now what works have we to show of such a kind as to give us "confidence," so that we may not "shrink from him in shame at his coming" (1 Jn 2:28).

According to Scripture, the self-denial which is the test of our faith must be daily. "If any man would come after me, let him deny himself and take up his cross daily and follow me" (Lk 9:23). It is thus that St. Luke records our Savior's words. Accordingly, it seems that Christian obedience does not consist merely in a few occasional efforts, a few accidental good deeds, or certain seasons of repentance, prayer, and activity. Again, the word daily implies that the self-denial which is pleasing to Christ consists in little things. This is plain, for opportunity for great self-denials does not come every day. Thus to take up the Cross of Christ is no great action done once for all, it consists in the continual practice of small duties which are distasteful to us.

If a person asks how he is to know whether he is dreaming on in the world's slumber or is really awake and alive unto God, let him first fix his mind upon some one or other of his besetting infirmities. Everyone who is at all in the habit of examining himself must be conscious of such within him. Many men have more than one, all of us have some one or other, and in resisting and overcoming such, self-denial has its first employment.

One man is indolent and fond of amusement, another man is passionate and ill-tempered, another is vain, another has little control over his tongue; others are weak and cannot resist the ridicule of thoughtless companions; others are tormented with bad passions. Let everyone consider what his weak point is: in that is his trial. His trial is not in those things which are easy to him, but in that one thing, in those several things, whatever they are, in which to do his duty is against his nature. Never think yourself safe because you do your duty in ninety-nine points; it is the hundredth which is to be the ground of your self-denial, which must evidence, or rather instance and realize your faith. It is in reference to this you must watch and pray, pray continually for God's grace to help you and watch with fear and trembling lest you fall.

Besides this, there are other modes of self-denial to try your faith and sincerity which it may be right just to mention. It may so happen that the sin you are most liable to is not called forth every day. For instance, anger and passion are irresistible perhaps when they come upon you, but it is only at times that you are provoked, and then you are off your guard, so that the occasion is over, and you have failed before you were well aware of its coming. It is right then almost to find out for yourself daily self-denials, and this because our Lord bids you take up your cross daily, and because it proves your earnestness, and because by doing so you strengthen your general power of self-mastery and come to have such an habitual command of yourself as will be a defense ready prepared when the season of temptation comes.

How are you to know you are in earnest? Make some sacrifice, do some distasteful thing which you are not actually obliged to do (so long as it is lawful) to bring home to your mind that in fact you do love your Savior, that you do hate sin, that you do hate your sinful nature, that you have put aside the present world. Thus you will have an evidence (to a certain point) that you are not using mere words. It is easy to make professions, easy to say fine things in speech or in writing, easy to astonish men with truths which they do not know and sentiments which rise above human nature. "But as for you, man of God, shun all this; aim at righteousness, godliness, faith, love, steadfastness, gentleness" (1 Tim 6:11). Let not your words run on. Try yourself daily in little deeds to prove that your faith is more than a deceit.

Saturday of the Second Week of Lent

Life the Season of Repentance

Is it not a common case for men and for women to neglect religion in their best days? They have been baptized; they have been taught their duty; they have been taught to pray; they know their Creed; they have opportunity to come to Church. This is their birthright, the privileges of their birth of water and of the Spirit, but they sell it as Esau did. They are tempted by Satan with some bribe of this world, and they give up their birthright in exchange for what is sure to perish and to make them perish with it. Esau was tempted by the mess of pottage which he saw in Jacob's hands. Satan arrested the eyes of his lust, and he gazed on the pottage as Eve gazed on the fruit of the tree of knowledge of good and evil. Adam and Eve sold their birthright for the fruit of a tree; Esau sold his for a mess of lentils. And men now-a-days often sell theirs, not indeed for anything so simple as fruit or herbs, but for some evil gain or other, which at the time they think worth purchasing at any price, perhaps for the enjoyment of some particular sin or more commonly for the indulgence of general carelessness. And thus they are profane persons, for they despise the great gift of God.

And then, when all is done and over, and their souls are sold to Satan, they never seem to understand that they have parted with their birthright. They think that they stand just where they did before they followed the world, the flesh, and the devil. They take for granted that when they choose to become more decent, or more religious, they have all their privileges just as before. And like Esau, instead of repenting for the loss of the birthright, they come, as a matter of course, for the blessing. Esau went out to hunt for venison gaily and promptly brought it to his father. His spirits were high; his voice was cheerful. It did not strike him that God was angry with him for what had passed years ago. He thought he was as sure of the blessing as if he had not sold the birthright.

And then, alas, the truth flashed upon him. He uttered a great and bitter cry when it was too late. It would have been well had he uttered it before he came for the blessing, not after it. He repented when it was too late. So it is for persons who have in any way sinned. It is good for them not to forget that they have sinned. It is good that they should lament and deplore their past sins. Depend upon it, they will wail over them in the next world, if they wail not here.

Would you see how a penitent should come to God? Turn to the parable of the Prodigal Son. He, too, had squandered away his birthright, as Esau did. He, too, came for the blessing, like Esau. But how differently he came. He came with deep confession and self-abasement. He said, "Father, I have sinned against heaven and before you; I am no longer worthy to be called your son; treat me as one of your hired servants" (Lk 15:18-19). But Esau said, "Let my father arise, and eat of his son's game, that you may bless me" (Gen 27:31). The one came for a son's privileges; the other for a servant's drudgery. The one killed and dressed his venison with his own hand and enjoyed it not; for the other the fatted calf was prepared and there was music and dancing.

These are thoughts especially suited to this season. From the earliest times down to this day, these weeks before Easter have been set apart every year for the particular remembrance and confession of our sins. From the first age downward, not a year has passed but Christians have been exhorted to reflect how far they have let go their birthright, as a preparation for claiming the blessing. At Christmas, we are born again with Christ. At Easter, we keep the eucharistic feast. In Lent, by penance, we join the two great sacraments together. Is there any single Christian alive who will dare to profess that he has not in greater or less degree sinned against God's free mercies as bestowed on him in baptism? Who will say that he has so improved his birthright that the blessing is his fit reward without sin to confess? Now it is that, God being your helper, you are to attempt to throw off from you the heavy burden of past transgression, to reconcile yourself to him who has once already imparted to you his atoning merits.

Such advice is especially suitable to an age like this when there is an effort on all hands to multiply comforts and to get rid of the daily inconveniences and distresses of life. Alas, how do you know, if you avail yourselves of the luxuries of this world without restraint, but that you are only postponing an inevitable chastisement? How do you know, but that, if you will not satisfy the debt of daily sin now, it will hereafter come upon you with interest? See whether this is not a thought which would spoil that enjoyment which even religious persons are apt to take in this world's goods, if they would but admit it. It is said that we ought to enjoy this life as the gift of God. Easy circumstances are generally thought a special happiness; it is thought a great point to get rid of annoyance or discomfort of mind and body; it is thought allowable and suitable to make use of all means available for making life pleasant. We desire, and confess we desire, to make time pass agreeably and to live in the sunshine. We aim at having all things at our will.

And thus year follows year, tomorrow as today, until we think that this, our artificial life, is our natural state and must and ever will be. But what if this fair weather but ensure the storm afterwards? What if it be that the nearer you attain to making yourself as a god on earth now, the greater pain lies before you in time to come, or even (if it must be said) the more certain becomes your ruin when time is at and end? Come down, then, from your high chamber at this season to avert what else may be. Let not the year go round and round without a break and interruption in its circle of pleasures. Give back some of God's gifts to God that you may safely enjoy the rest. Fast or watch or abound in alms, or deny yourselves society or pleasant books or easy clothing, or take on you some irksome task or employment: do one or other or some or all of these, unless you say that you have never sinned and may go like Esau with a light heart to take your crown. Ever bear in mind that Day which will reveal all things and will test all things "through fire" (1 Cor 3:15) and which will bring us into judgment ere it lodges us in heaven.

Third Sunday of Lent

Christ, the Son of God Made Man

From eternity, Christ was the Living and True God: "Before Abraham was, I am" (Jn 8:58). By these words he declares that he did not begin to exist from the Virgin's womb but had been in existence before. And by using the words "I am," he seems to allude to the Name of God, which was revealed to Moses in the burning bush, when he was commanded to say to the children of Israel, "I am has sent me to you" (Ex 3:14). In like manner St. John says, "In the beginning was the Word, and the Word was with God, and the Word was God" (Jn 1:1). St. Thomas addresses him as his Lord and his God (Jn 20:28), and St. Paul declares that he is "God over all, blessed for ever" (Rom 9:5). We know, indeed, that the Father is God also, and so is the Holy Spirit, but still Christ is God and Lord, most fully, completely, and entirely, in all attributes as perfect and as adorable, as if nothing had been told us of Father or of Holy Spirit, as much to be adored, as, before he came in the flesh, the Father was adored by the Jews, and is now to be adored by us "in spirit and truth" (Jn 4:23). For he tells us expressly himself, "He who has seen me has seen the Father" (Jn 14:9), and that "all may honor the Son, even as they honor the Father" (Jn 5:23).

Our Lord was not only God, but the Son of God. We know more than that God took on him our flesh. Though all is mysterious, we have a point of knowledge further and more distinct: that it was neither the Father nor the Holy Spirit, but the Son of the Father, God the Son, God from God, and Light from Light, who came down upon earth, and who thus, though graciously taking on him a new nature, remained in person as he had been from everlasting, the Son of the Father, and spoke and acted towards the Father as a Son.

As the Son was God, so was the Son suitably made man. It belonged to him to assume a servant's form. While They are one in substance, each of the Persons of the Ever-Blessed and All-Holy Trinity has distinct characteristics which the Other has not. The Son of God was a Son both before his incarnation, and, by a second mystery, after it. From eternity, he had been the only-begotten in the bosom of the Father, and when he came on earth, this essential relation to the Father remained unaltered. He was a Son when in the form of a servant, still performing the will of the Father, as his Father's Word and Wisdom, manifesting his Father's glory and accomplishing his Father's purposes.

When the Son of God took our nature upon him, he acted through it without ceasing to be what he was before, making it but the instrument of his gracious purposes. It must not be supposed because it was an instrument that therefore it was not intimately one with him. Far from it. Though his divine nature was sovereign and supreme when he became incarnate, yet the manhood which he assumed was not kept at a distance from him as a mere instrument, or put on as a mere garment, or entered as a mere tabernacle, but it was really taken into the closest and most ineffable union with him.

All that he did and said on earth was but the immediate deed and word of God the Son acting by means of his human tabernacle. He surrounded himself with it. He lodged it within him, and thenceforth the Eternal Word, the Son of God, the Second Person in the Blessed Trinity, had two natures, the one his own as really as the other, divine and human. And he acted through both of them, sometimes through both at once, sometimes through One and not through the other, as Almighty God acts sometimes by the attribute of justice, sometimes by that of love, sometimes through both together. He was as entirely man as if he had ceased to be God, as fully God as if he had never become man, as fully both at once as he was in being at all.

The Athanasian Creed expresses all this as follows: "The right faith is that we believe and confess that our Lord Jesus Christ the Son of God is God and man; God of the substance of his Father, begotten before the worlds, and man of the substance of his Mother, born in the world. Perfect God and perfect man, of a reasonable soul and human flesh subsisting: who, although he be God and man, yet is not two but one Christ. One, not by conversion of the Godhead into flesh," as if he could cease to be God, "but by taking of the manhood into God," taking it into his divine person as his own. "One altogether, not by confusion of substance," not by the divine nature and the human becoming some new nature, as if he ceased to be God, and did not become a man, "but by unity of person." This is what his unity consists in: he who came on earth was the very Same who had been from everlasting.

We ought not to speak, we ought not to hear, such high truths, without great reverence and awe and preparation of mind. And this is a reason, perhaps, why this is a proper season for dwelling on them, when we have been engaged, not in mirth and festivity, but in chastening and sobering ourselves. The Psalmist says, "O Lord, my heart is not lifted up, my eyes are not raised too high; I do not occupy myself with things too great and too marvelous for me. But I have calmed and quieted my soul, like a child quieted at its mother's breast; like a child that is quieted is my soul" (Ps 131:1-2). When we are engaged in weaning ourselves from this world, when we are denying ourselves even lawful things, when we have a subdued tone of thought and feeling, then is an allowable time to speak of the high mysteries of the faith. And then, too, are they especially a comfort to us. Those who neglect fasting make light of orthodoxy too. But to those who through God's grace are otherwise minded, the Creed of the Church brings relief, when, amid the gloom of their own hearts, Christ rises like the Sun of righteousness, giving them peace for disquiet, "to give them a garland instead of ashes, the oil of gladness instead of mourning, the mantle of praise instead of a faint spirit; that they may be called oaks of righteousness, the planting of the Lord, that he may be glorified" (Is 61:3).

Monday of the Third Week of Lent

Endurance of the World's Censure

This world is a scene of conflict between good and evil. The evil not only avoids but persecutes the good; the good cannot conquer except by suffering. Good men seem to fail. Their cause triumphs, but their own overthrow is the price paid for the success of their cause. When was it that this conflict and this character and issue of it have not been fulfilled? So it was in the beginning. Cain was envious of his brother Abel and slew him. Joseph's brethren were filled with bitter hatred of him, debated about killing him, cast him into a pit, and at last sold him into Egypt. The chief priests and Pharisees, full of envy, rose up against our Lord Jesus Christ and delivered him to the heathen governor to be crucified. So the apostles after him, and especially St. Paul, were persecuted by their fierce and revengeful countrymen, and from the way in which St. Paul speaks on the subject we may infer that it is ever so to be: "all who desire to live a godly life in Christ Jesus will be persecuted" (2 Tim 3:12). Hence our Savior, to console all who suffer for his sake, graciously says, "Blessed are those who are persecuted for righteousness' sake, for theirs is the kingdom of heaven" (Mt 5:10).

The case seems to be this: those who do not serve God with a single heart know that they ought to do so, and they do not like to be reminded that they ought. And when they fall in with anyone who does live to God, he serves to remind them of it, and that is unpleasant to them, and that is the reason why they are angry with a religious man: the sight of him disturbs them and makes them uneasy. Accordingly, they do all they can to believe that he is making a pretense of religion. They do their utmost to find out what looks like inconsistency in him and call him a hypocrite. Christians are called names, untruths are told of them, they are ridiculed, and men encourage each other to oppose them and to deceive them. And why? For this simple reason: because they are God's messengers, and men in general do not like to be told of God.

You must, therefore, learn to cherish patience and resignation, when the world scorns you for your religion, and learn to bear your cross lightly, and not gloomily, or sadly, or complainingly.

People may press you to do something which you know to be wrong—to tell an untruth, or to do what is not quite honest, or to go where you should not go—and they may show that they are vexed at the notion of your not complying. Still you must not comply. You must not do what you feel to be wrong, though you should thereby displease even those whom you would most wish to please.

Again, you must not be surprised should you find that you are called a hypocrite and other hard names; you must not mind it.

Again, you may discover to your great vexation that untruths are told of you by careless persons behind your backs, that what you do has been misrepresented, and that in consequence a number of evil things are believed about you by the world at large. Hard though it be, you must not care for it, remembering that more untruths were told of our Savior and his apostles than can possibly be told of you.

In many, very many ways, you may be called upon to bear the ill-usage of the world or to withstand its attempts to draw you from God, but you must be firm, and you must not be surprised that they should be made. You must consider that it is your very calling to bear and to withstand. This is what you offer to God as a sort of return for his great mercies to you. Did not Christ go through much more for you than you can possibly be called upon to undergo for him? Did he bear the bitter cross who was sinless, and do you, who are at best so sinful, scruple to bear such poor trials and petty inconveniences?

Nevertheless, do not be too eager to suppose you are ill-treated for your religion's sake. Make as light of matters as you can. And beware of being severe on those who lead careless lives, or whom you think or know to be ill-treating you. Do not dwell on such matters. Turn your mind away from them. Avoid all gloominess. Be kind and gentle to those who are perverse, and you will very often gain them over. You should pray for those who lead careless lives and especially if they are unkind to you. Who knows but God may hear your prayers and turn their hearts? Do everything for them but imitate them and yield to them. This is the true Christian spirit, to be meek and gentle under ill-usage, cheerful under slander, forgiving towards enemies, and silent in the midst of angry tongues.

Secondly, recollect that you cannot do any one thing of these duties without God's help. Anyone who attempts to resist the world or to do other good things by his own strength will surely fail. We can do good things, but it is when God gives us power to do them. Therefore, we must pray to him for the power. When we are brought into temptation of any kind, we should lift up our hearts to God. We should say to him, "Good Lord, deliver us." The disciples, when Christ went, had to go through much trouble, and therefore he comforted them by the coming of the Holy Spirit. "I have said this to you, that in me you may have peace. In the world you have tribulation; but be of good cheer, I have overcome the world" (Jn 16:33).

Lastly, none of us, even the best, have resisted the world as we ought to have done. Our faces have not been like flints. We have been afraid of men's words and dismayed by their looks, and we have yielded to them at times against our better judgment. We have fancied the world could do us some harm while we kept to the commandments of God. Let us search our consciences. Let us look back on our past lives. Let us try to purify and cleanse our hearts in God's sight. Let us try to live more like Christians, more like children of God. Let us earnestly beg of God to teach us more simply and clearly what our duty is. Let us beg of him to give us the heart to love him and true repentance for what is past. Let us beg him to teach us how to confess him before men, lest if we deny him now, he should deny us before the angels of God hereafter.

Tuesday of the Third Week of Lent

Dangers to the Penitent

No state is more dreary than that of the repentant sinner, when first he understands where he is and begins to turn his thoughts towards his Great Master whom he has offended. Of course, it is tempered with comfort and hope, as are all acts of duty. But at the time it is a most dreary state. A man finds that he has a great work to do and does not know how to do it, or even what it is, and his impatience and restlessness are as great as his conscious ignorance.

Repentant sinners are often impatient to put themselves upon some new line of action or to adopt some particular rule of life. They feel that what they have done in time past is, as far as this life is concerned, indelible, and places an impassable barrier between themselves and others. They feel that they can never be as others are, till the voice of Christ pronounces them acquitted and blessed. And their heart yearns towards humiliation and burns with a godly indignation against themselves, as if nothing were too bad for them; and they look about for something to do, some state of life to engage in, some task or servile office to undertake.

Now it commonly happens that God does not disclose his will to them at once, and for that will they ought to wait. St. Paul should be the pattern of the true penitent here. It was not till years after his conversion that the Holy Spirit said, "Set apart for me Barnabas and Saul for the work to which I have called them" (Acts 13:2). What a lesson is this for patient waiting on God! "Wait for the Lord" (Ps 27:14), wait till he speaks. Never regard how long you have to wait; be it for years, suffer it. Say not time is short, for God can make it long.

When persons are in acute distress about their sins, they are sometimes tempted to make rash promises, and to take on them professions without counting the cost. They think their present state of mind will last forever. It changes, but their promise remains. They find they cannot duly fulfil it; then they are in great perplexity, and even despair. Perhaps they have been even imprudent enough to make their engagement in the shape of a vow, and this greatly increases their difficulty. They do not know whether it is binding or no. They cannot recollect the mode in which, or the feelings under which, they took it, or any of the minute circumstances on which its validity turns. Now all this on the very first view of the case shows thus much, how very wrong it is to make private vows. We cannot be our own judge in a matter of this kind. Yet, if we take on ourselves an engagement without telling anyone else of it, we trust it in a great measure to our own memory and judgment. The special publicity and distinctness with which the marriage vow is made gives us a pattern how vows should be undertaken. The Church should hear them, and the Church should bless them.

There is something which persons may do, which will practically come to the same thing, yet without the risk of their acting on their own judgment, unaccompanied by the formal blessing of the Church on their act. They may make it a point ever to pray God for that gift or that state which they covet. If they desire to be humble and of little account in this world, let them not at once make any engagement or profession to that effect, but let them daily pray God that they may never be rich, never be in high place, never in power or authority. Let them daily pray God that their dwelling may be ever lowly, their food ordinary, their apparel common, their home solitary. Let them pray him that they may be least and lowest in the world's society, that others may have precedence of them, others speak while they are silent, others take the first seats, and they the last, others receive deference, and they neglect. Will not such a prayer be a sort of recurrent vow, yet without any of that dangerous boldness which a private self-devised resolution implies? Who can go on day by day thus praying, yet not imbibe somewhat of the spirit for which he prays?

When men are in the first fervor of penitence, they should be careful not to act on their own private judgment, and without proper advice. Not only in forming lasting engagements, but in all they do, they need a calmer guidance than their own. They cannot manage themselves; they must be guided by others; the neglect of this simple and natural rule leads to very evil consequences. We should all of us be saved a great deal of suffering of various kinds, if we could but persuade ourselves, that we are not the best judges, whether of our own condition, or of God's will towards us. What sensible person undertakes to be his own physician? Yet are the diseases of the mind less numerous, less intricate, less subtle than those of the body? Is experience of no avail in things spiritual as well as in things material?

Nothing healthy can be expected in religion till we learn that we cannot by our private judgment manage ourselves, that management of the heart is a science, and that even though we have paid attention to it, we are least able to exercise it in our own case, that is, then when we most need it. We must use in religious matters that common sense, which does not desert us in matters of this world because we take a real interest in them. And as no one would ever dream of being his own lawyer or his own physician, so we must take it for granted, if we would serve God comfortably, that we cannot be our own theologians and our own confessors.

Let us excite each other to seek that good part which shall not be taken away from us. Let us labor to be really in earnest and to view things in the way in which God views them. Then it will be but a little thing to give up the world. Let us turn our mind heavenward, and in his own time God will set our affections there also. Let the time past suffice us to have followed our own will. Let us desire to form part of that glorious company of apostles and prophets, of whom we read in Scripture. Let us cast in our lot with them and desire to be gathered together under their feet. Let us beg of God to employ us. Let us try to obtain a spirit of perfect self-surrender to him and an indifference to one thing above another in this world, so that we may be ready to follow his call whenever it comes to us. Thus shall we best employ ourselves till his voice is heard, patiently preparing for it by meditation and looking for him to perfect what we trust his own grace has begun in us.

Wednesday of the Third Week of Lent

Apostolic Abstinence a Pattern for Christians

"No longer drink only water, but use a little wine for the sake of your stomach and your frequent ailments" (1 Tim 5:23). This remarkable verse was addressed to Timothy, St. Paul's companion, the first Bishop of Ephesus. Of Timothy we know very little, except that he did minister to St. Paul, and hence we might have inferred that he was a man of very saintly character. St. Paul says to the Philippians, that he has "no one like" Timothy, who would "be genuinely anxious for your welfare" (Phil 2:20). This is but a general account of him, and we seem to desire something more definite in the way of description beyond merely knowing that he was a great saint, which conveys no clear impression to the mind. But here we have a glimpse given us of his mode of life. St. Paul does not expressly tell us that he was a man of mortified habits, but he reveals the fact indirectly by cautioning him against an excess of mortification. "No longer drink only water," he says, "but use a little wine." It should be observed that wine, in the southern countries, is the same ordinary beverage that beer is here; it is nothing strong or costly. Yet even from such as this, Timothy was in the habit of abstaining, and restricting himself to water; and, as the apostle thought, imprudently, to the increase of his "frequent ailments." So, this holy man, without impiously disparaging God's creation and thanklessly rejecting God's gifts, yet, on the whole, lived a life of abstinence.

At first sight it may not be clear why this moderation, and at least occasional abstinence, in the use of God's gifts, should be so great a duty as our Lord seems to imply when he places fasting in so prominent a place in the Sermon on the Mount, with almsgiving and prayer. But thus much we are able to see, that the great duty of the Gospel is love to God and man, and that this love is quenched and extinguished by self-indulgence and cherished by self-denial. They who enjoy this life freely make it or self their idol; they are gross-hearted and have no eyes to see God. Hence it is said, "Blessed are the pure in heart, for they shall see God" (Mt 5:8). And again, it was the rich man who fared sumptuously every day, who neglected Lazarus; for sensual living hardens the heart, while abstinence softens and refines it. Abstinence does not produce this effect as a matter of course in any given person, else all the poor ought to be patterns of Christian love, but where men are religiously-minded, there those out of the number will make greater attainments in love and devotional feeling, who do exercise themselves in self-denial of the body.

Love is no common grace in its higher degrees. It is true, indeed, that, as being the necessary token of every true Christian, it must be possessed in some degree even by the weakest and humblest of Christ's servants—but in any of its higher and maturer stages, it is rare and difficult. It is easy to be amiable or upright. It is easy to live in regular habits. It is easy to live conscientiously, in the common sense of the word. All this is comparatively easy. But one thing is needful, and one thing is often lacking: love. We may act rightly, yet without doing our right actions from the love of God. Other motives, short of love, are good in themselves; these we may have, and not have love. Now this defect does not arise from any one cause, nor can it be removed by any one remedy, and yet still, it does seem as if abstinence and fasting availed much towards its removal; so much so, that, granting love is necessary, then these are necessary. Assuming love to be the characteristic of a Christian, so is abstinence. You may think to dispense with fasting; true; and you may neglect also to cultivate love.

Here a connection may be traced between this truth and our Lord's words, when asked why his disciples did not fast. He said, that they could not fast while the Bridegroom was with them, but that when he was taken from them, then they would fast (see Mt 9:15). The one thing, which is all in all to us, is to live in Christ's presence, to hear his voice, to see his countenance. His first disciples had him in bodily presence among them, and he spoke to them, warned them, was a pattern to them, and guided them with his eye. But when he withdrew himself from the world of sense, how should they see him still? When their fleshly eyes and ears saw him no more, when he had ascended to where flesh and blood cannot enter, and the barrier of the flesh was interposed between him and them, how should they any longer see and hear him? "Lord, where are you going?" they said. And he answered to Peter, "Where I am going you cannot follow me now; but you shall follow afterward" (Jn 13:36). They were to follow him through the veil and to break the barrier of the flesh after his pattern. They must, as far as they could, weaken and attenuate what stood between them and him. They must anticipate that world where flesh and blood are not; they must discern truths which flesh and blood could not reveal; they must live a life, not of sense, but of spirit. They must practice those mortifications which the Pharisees and John's disciples observed, with better fruit, for a higher end, in a more heavenly way, in order to see him who is invisible. By fasting, Moses saw God's glory; by fasting, Elijah heard the "still small voice" (1 Kings 19:12). By fasting, Christ's disciples were to express their mourning over the Crucified and Dead, over the Bridegroom taken away, but that mourning would bring him back, that mourning would be turned to joy. In that mourning they would see him, they would hear of him, for "blessed are those who mourn, for they shall be comforted" (Mt 5:4). They are "sorrowful, yet always rejoicing" (2 Cor 6:10), hungering and thirsting after righteousness, fasting in body, that they may be satisfied in spirit, and in a "dry and weary land where no water is" (Ps 63:1), that they may look for him in holiness and behold his power and glory.

Such was the portion which St. Paul and St. Timothy received when they gave up this world and its blessings, not that they might not have enjoyed them had they chosen, but because they might, and yet gave them up, therefore they received blessings out of sight instead. In like manner, applying this to ourselves, it is our duty also to be ever moderate, and at times to abstain, in the use of God's earthly gifts. It is our duty to war against the flesh as they warred against it, that we may inherit the gifts of the Spirit as they inherited them.

Thursday of the Third Week of Lent

Curiosity a Temptation to Sin

One chief cause of wickedness which is everywhere seen in the world is our curiosity to have some fellowship with darkness, some experience of sin, to know what the pleasures of sin are like. It is even thought a thing to be ashamed of to have no knowledge of sin by experience, as if it argued a strange seclusion from the world, a childish ignorance of life, a narrowness of mind, and a superstitious, slavish fear. Not to know sin by experience brings upon a man the laughter and jests of his companions. Nor is it wonderful this should be the case in the descendants of that guilty pair to whom Satan in the beginning held out admittance into a strange world of knowledge and enjoyment as the reward of disobedience to God's commandment. A discontent with the abundance of blessings which were given, because something was withheld, was the sin of our first parents. In like manner, a wanton roving after things forbidden, a curiosity to know what it was to be as the heathen, was one chief source of the idolatries of the Jews, and we at this day inherit with them a like nature from Adam.

Curiosity strangely moves us to disobedience in order that we may have experience of the pleasure of disobedience. We intrude into things forbidden: in reading what we should not read, in hearing what we should not hear, in seeing what we should not see, in going into company where we should not go, in presumptuous reasonings and arguing when we should have faith, in acting as if we were our own masters where we should obey. We indulge our reason, our passions, our ambition, our vanity, our love of power, and all the while we think that, after having acquired this miserable knowledge of good and evil, we can return to our duty and continue where we left off.

Now this delusion arises from Satan, the father of lies, who knows well that if he can get us once to sin, he can easily make us sin twice and thrice, till at length we are taken captive at his will (see 2 Tim 2:26). He sees that curiosity is man's great and first snare, as it was in paradise. His plan of action then lies plain before him: to tempt us violently, while the world is new to us and our hopes and feelings are eager and restless. Hence is seen the Divine wisdom, as well as the merciful consideration, of the advice contained in Scripture: "Do not enter the path of the wicked, and do not walk in the way of evil men. Avoid it; do not go on it; turn away from it and pass on" (Prov 4:14-15).

Let us give our minds to the consideration of this plain truth: the great thing in religion is to set off well, to resist the beginnings of sin, to flee temptation, to avoid the company of the wicked.

First, because it is hardly possible to delay our flight without rendering flight impossible. Whatever the temptation may be, there may be no time to wait and gaze without being caught. Woe to us if Satan sees us first, so to say, for as in the case of some beast of prey, for him to see us is to master us. Directly we are made aware of the temptation, we shall, if we are wise, turn our backs upon it, without waiting to think and reason about it. There are temptations when this advice is especially necessary, but under all it is highly seasonable.

Consider what must in all cases be the consequence of allowing evil thoughts to be present to us, though we do not actually admit them into our hearts: we shall make ourselves familiar with them. Now our great security against sin lies in being shocked at it. Thus, for instance, everyone is shocked at cursing and swearing when he first hears it, and at first he cannot help even showing that he is shocked. But when he has once got accustomed to such profane talking and been laughed out of his strictness, then he soon learns to defend it. He says he means no harm by it, that it does no one any harm, that it is only so many words, and that everybody uses them. Here is an instance in which disobedience to what we know to be right makes us blind.

But there is another wretched effect of sinning once which sometimes takes place: being so seduced by it as forthwith to continue in the commission of it ever afterwards, without seeking for arguments to meet our conscience, from a mere headstrong greediness after its bad pleasures. There are beasts of prey which are said to abstain from blood till they taste it, but once tasting it, ever seek it. In like manner, there is a sort of thirst for sin which is born with us, but which grace quenches, and which is thus kept under till we, by our own act, rouse it again, and which, once aroused, never can be allayed. We sin, while we confess that the wages of sin is death.

Now to what do considerations such as these lead us, but to our Lord's simple and comprehensive precept: "Watch and pray that you may not enter into temptation" (Mt 26:41). To enter not the path of the wicked, to avoid it and pass it by, what is this but the exercise of watching? Therefore, he insists upon it so much, knowing that in it our safety lies. We are told that our "adversary the devil prowls around like a roaring lion, seeking some one to devour," and therefore are warned to "be sober, be watchful" (1 Pet 5:8). And assuredly, our true comfort lies not in disguising the truth from ourselves, but in knowing something more than this: that though Satan is against us, God is for us and that in every temptation he will make a way for us to escape.

Sinners think that they know all that religion has to give, and over and above that they know the pleasures of sin, too. No, they do not, cannot, never will know the secret gift of God, till they repent and amend. They never will know what it is to see God till they obey. They never will know the blessedness which he has to give. They do know the satisfaction of sinning, such as it is, and alas, if they go on as they are going, they will know not only what sin is but what hell is. But they never will know that great secret which is hid in the Father and in the Son.

Let us not be seduced by the Tempter and his promises. He can show us no good. He has no good to give us. Rather, let us listen to the gracious words of our Maker and Redeemer: "Call to me and I will answer you, and will tell you great and hidden things which you have not known" (Jer 33:3).

Friday of the Third Week of Lent

Faith and Love

What is charity? St. Paul answers by giving a great number of properties of it, all distinct and special. It is patient, it is kind, it has no envy, no self-importance, no ostentation, no indecorum, no selfishness, no irritability, no malevolence. Which of all these is it? For if it is all at once, surely it is a name for all virtues at once.

And what makes this conclusion still more plausible is that St. Paul elsewhere actually calls charity "the fulfilling of the law" (Rom 13:10), and our Savior, in like manner, makes our whole duty consist in loving God and loving our neighbor. St. James calls it "the royal law" (Jas 2:8), and St. John says, "We know that we have passed out of death into life, because we love the brethren" (1 Jn 3:14).

It is well too, by way of contrast, to consider the description of faith given elsewhere by St. Paul. In his Epistle to the Hebrews, he devotes a much longer chapter to it, but his method of treating it is altogether different. He starts with a definition of it, and then he illustrates his clear and precise account of it in a series of instances. The chapter is made up of a repetition—in Noah, in Abraham, in Moses, in David, and in the Prophets—of one and the same precisely marked excellence called faith, which is such as no one can mistake. Again, he mentions it elsewhere, in the midst of a train of thought altogether different but with a description that agrees with what is said in Hebrews: "faith, so as to remove mountains" (1 Cor 13:2), which moreover is the very account of it given by our Lord and expresses surely the same habit of mind as that by which Noah, Abraham, Moses, and David preached righteousness, obtained promises, renounced the world, waxed valiant in fight. How then is it that faith is of so definite a character and love so large and comprehensive?

The reason seems to be pretty much what at first sight is the difficulty. The difficulty is whether, if love be such as St. Paul describes, it is not all virtues at once, and, in one sense, it is all virtues at once, and therefore St. Paul cannot describe it more definitely, more restrictedly than he does. In other words, it is the root of all holy dispositions, and grows and blossoms into them. They are its parts, and when it is described, they of necessity are mentioned. Love is the material out of which all graces are made, the quality of mind which is the fruit of regeneration, and in which the Spirit dwells, according to St. John's words, "he who loves is born of God . . . and he who abides in love abides in God, and God abides in him" (1 Jn 4:7, 16). Such is love, and, as being such, it will last forever. "Love never ends" (1 Cor 13:8).

Faith and hope are graces of an imperfect state, and they cease with that state, but love is greater, because it is perfection. Faith and hope are graces, as far as we belong to this world, which is for a time. But love is a grace because we are creatures of God whether here or elsewhere and partakers in a redemption which is to last forever. Faith will not be when there is sight, nor hope when there is enjoyment, but love will increase more and more to all eternity. Faith and hope are means by which we express our love. We believe God's word because we love it; we hope after heaven because we love it. We should not have any hope or concern about it unless we loved it. We should not trust or confide in the God of heaven unless we loved him. Faith, then, and hope are but instruments or expressions of love. But as to love itself: we do not love because we believe, for the devils believe yet do not love. Nor do we love because we hope, for hypocrites hope, who do not love. But we love for no cause beyond itself. We love because it is our nature to love, and it is our nature because God the Holy Spirit has made it our nature. Love is the immediate fruit and the evidence of regeneration.

Faith at most makes us a hero. Love makes a saint. Faith can put us above the world, but love brings us under God's throne. Faith can make us sober, but love makes us happy. It is possible for a man to have the clearest, calmest, most exact view of the realities of heaven, may most firmly realize and act upon the truths of the Gospel, may understand that all about him is but a veil, may have that full confidence in God's word as to be able to do miracles, may have such simple, absolute faith as to give up his property to feed the poor, may so scorn the world and with so royal a heart trample upon it as even to give his body to be burned by a glorious martyrdom, and yet it is abstractedly possible, that not one of these proper acts of faith in itself necessarily implies love. The apostle says that though a person be all that has been said, yet unless he be also something besides, unless he have love, it profits him nothing. O fearful lesson to all those who are tempted to pride themselves in their labors or sufferings or sacrifices or works! We are Christ's, not by faith merely, nor by works merely, but by love. Not by hating the world, nor by hating sin, nor by venturing for the world to come, nor by calmness, nor by magnanimity—though we must do and be all this—but it is love that makes faith, not faith love. We are saved, not by any of these things, but by that heavenly flame within us, which, while it consumes what is seen aspires to what is unseen. Love is the gentle, tranquil, satisfied acquiescence and adherence of the soul in the contemplation of God. Not only a preference of God before all things, but a delight in him because he is God. Not any violent emotion or transport, but, as St. Paul describes it, long-suffering, kind, modest, unassuming, innocent, simple, orderly, disinterested, meek, pure-hearted, sweet-tempered, patient, enduring. Faith without charity is dry, harsh, and sapless; it has nothing sweet, engaging, winning, soothing. It was charity which brought Christ down. Charity is but another name for the Comforter. It is eternal Charity which is the bond of all things in heaven and earth. It is Charity wherein the Father and the Son are one in the unity of the Spirit, by which the angels in heaven are one, by which all saints are one with God, by which the Church is one upon earth.

Saturday of the Third Week of Lent

Times of Private Prayer

The Pharisees were in the practice, when they prayed by themselves, of praying in public, in the corners of the streets. Public private prayer: this was their self-contradictory practice. Warning, then, his disciples against the particular form of hypocrisy in which the self-conceit of human nature at that day showed itself, our Lord promises his Father's blessing on such humble supplications as were really addressed to him and not made to gain the praise of men: "when you pray, go into your room and shut the door and pray to your Father who is in secret; and your Father who sees in secret will reward you" (Mt 6:6). Those who seek the unseen God, he seems to say, seek him in their hearts and hidden thoughts, not in loud words, as if he were far off from them. Such men would retire from the world into places where no human eye saw them, there to meet him humbly and in faith. And he, the searcher of hearts, would reward them openly. Prayers uttered in secret, according to God's will, are treasured up in God's Book of Life. They seem, perhaps, to have sought an answer here and to have failed. Their memory perishes even in the mind of the petitioner, and the world never knew of them. But God is ever mindful, and in the last day, when the books are opened, they shall be disclosed and rewarded before the whole world.

Such is Christ's gracious promise. He acknowledges and blesses, in his condescension, those devotional exercises which were a duty even before Scripture enjoined them, and, changing into a privilege that work of faith, which, though bidden by conscience and authorized by reason, yet before he revealed his mercy is laden in every man's case who attempts it with guilt, remorse, and fear. It is the Christian's unspeakable privilege, and his alone, that he has at all times free access to the throne of grace through the mediation of his Lord and Savior.

Now, we know well enough that we are bound to be in one sense in prayer and meditation all the day long. The question then arises: are we to pray in any other way? Is it enough to keep our minds fixed upon God through the day and to commune with him in our hearts, or is it necessary, over and above this habitual faith, to set apart particular times for the more systematic and earnest exercise of it?

The practice of good men in Scripture gives us an example of it, and even our Savior had his peculiar seasons of communing with God. His thoughts indeed were one continued sacred service offered up to his Father. Nevertheless, we read of his going up "into the hills by himself to pray" (Mt 14:23), and, again, that "all night he continued in prayer to God" (Lk 6:12). St. Peter, too, as in the narrative of the conversion of Cornelius, the Roman centurion, in the tenth chapter of the Acts, went up upon the housetop to pray about the sixth hour, and God visited him. And Nathanael seems to have been in prayer under the fig tree, at the time our Savior saw him, and Philip called him (Jn 1:48). Instances from Scripture of such Israelites without guile are easily multiplied. The Psalmist says, "Seven times a day I praise you for your righteous ordinances" (Ps 119:164). And Daniel's practice is told us on a memorable occasion: "When Daniel knew that the document had been signed"—the impious decree forbidding prayer to any but king Darius—"he went to his house where he had windows in his upper chamber open toward Jerusalem; and he got down upon his knees three times a day and prayed and gave thanks before his God, as he had done previously" (Dan 6:10).

It is plain that besides the devotional temper in which we should pass the day, more solemn and direct acts of worship, nay, regular and periodical, are required of us by the precept of Christ, by his own example, and by that of his apostles and prophets.

Be sure, whoever of you is persuaded to disuse his morning and evening prayers is giving up the armor which is to secure him against the wiles of the Devil. Beware of the subtlety of your enemy, who would willingly rob you of your defense. Do not yield to his bad reasonings. Be on your guard especially when you get into novel situations or circumstances which interest and delight you, lest they throw you out of your regularity in prayer. Anything new or unexpected is dangerous to you. Going much into mixed society and seeing many strange persons, taking share in any pleasant amusements, reading interesting books, entering into a new line of life, forming some new acquaintance, the sudden prospect of any worldly advantage, traveling: all these things and such like, innocent as they are in themselves and capable of a religious use, become means of temptation if we are not on our guard. See that you are not unsettled by them; this is the danger.

Consider that stability of mind is the chief of virtues, for it is faith. "You keep him in perfect peace, whose mind is stayed on you, because he trusts in you" (Is 26:3); this is the promise. "But the wicked are like the tossing sea; for it cannot rest, and its waters toss up mire and dirt. There is no peace, says my God, for the wicked" (Is 57:20-21). Not to the wicked only, in our common sense of the word, but to none there is rest who in any way leave their God and rove after the goods of this world. Do not indulge visions of earthly good. Fix your hearts on higher things. Let your morning and evening thoughts be points of rest for your mind's eye, and let these thoughts be upon the narrow way, and the blessedness of heaven, and the glory and power of Christ your Savior. Thus will you be kept from unseemly risings and fallings, and steadied in an equable way. Men in general will know nothing of this. They witness not your private prayers, and they will confuse you with the multitude they fall in with. But your friends and acquaintances will gain a light and a comfort from your example. They will see your good works and be led to trace them to their true secret source, the influences of the Holy Spirit sought and obtained by prayer. Thus they will glorify your heavenly Father, and in imitation of you will seek him, and he who sees in secret shall at length reward you openly.

Fourth Sunday of Lent

Illuminating Grace

In order to see the truths of revelation, you need light. Not even the keenest eyes can see in the dark. Now, though your mind be the eye, the grace of God is the light, and you will as easily exercise your eyes in this sensible world without the sun, as you will be able to exercise your mind in the spiritual world without a parallel gift from without.

A blind man may pick up a good deal of information of various kinds, and be very conversant with the objects of sight, though he does not see. He may be able to talk about them fluently and may be fond of doing so; he may even talk of seeing as if he really saw, till he almost seems to pretend to the faculty of sight. If you ask how this comes about, it is partly because he hears what other men say about these things, and he is able to imitate them, and partly because he cannot help reasoning upon the things he hears and drawing conclusions from them. His words are tolerably correct and do not at once betray how little he knows what he is talking about. He infers one thing from another, and thus is able to speak of many things which he does not see, but only perceives must be so, granting other things are so. For instance, if he knows that blue and yellow make green, he may pronounce, without a chance of mistake, that green is more like blue than yellow is. It is not that he judges by sight, but that reason takes the place of it.

The natural man can feel, he can imagine, he can admire, he can reason, he can infer. In all these ways he may proceed to receive the whole or part of Catholic truth, but he cannot see, he cannot love.

The world tells us that certainty, and confidence, and boldness in speech are unchristian. Is this pleading a cause or a judgment from facts? Was the religion of Christ propagated by the vehemence of faith and love, or by a philosophical balance of arguments? Look back at the early martyrs. What were they? They were very commonly youths and maidens, soldiers and slaves: a set of hot-headed youth, who would have lived to be wise, had they not been obstinately set on dying first, who tore down imperial manifestoes, broke the peace, challenged the judges to dispute, would not rest till they got into the same den with a lion, and who, if chased out of one city, began preaching in another! So said the blind world about those who saw the Unseen. Yes, it was the spiritual sight of God which made them what they were. No one is a martyr for a conclusion; no one is a martyr for an opinion. It is faith that makes martyrs.

He who knows and loves the things of God has no power to deny them. He may have a natural shrinking from torture and death, but such terror is incommensurate with faith, and as little acts upon it as dust and mire touch the sun's light, or scents or voices could stop a wheel in motion. The martyrs saw, and how could they but speak what they had seen? They might shudder at the pain, but they had not the power not to see. If threats could undo the heavenly truths, then might pain silence their confession of them. The world is inquiring and large-minded, and knows many things; it talks well and profoundly. But is there one among its Babel of religious opinions which it would be a martyr for?

The world cannot believe that Catholics really hold what they profess to hold, and supposes that, if they are educated, they are kept up to their profession by external influence, by superstitious fear, by pride, by interest, or other bad or unworthy motive. Men of the world have never believed in their whole life, never have had simple faith in things unseen, never have had more than an opinion about them, and in consequence they think an absolute, unhesitating faith in anything unseen to be simply an extravagance, and especially when it is exercised on objects which they do not believe themselves, or even reject with scorn or abhorrence. They cannot understand how our faith in the Blessed Sacrament is a genuine, living portion of our minds. They think it a mere profession which we embrace with no inward assent, but only because we are told that we should be lost unless we profess it. But if we are to believe anything at all, if we are to make any one heavenly doctrine our own, if we are to take some dogmas as true, why, in that case, it should be a burden to believe what is so gracious and what so concerns us, rather than what is less intimate and less winning. Why we may not believe that God dwells on our altars as well as that he dwells in the sky certainly is not so self-evident.

Oh, how narrow-minded is this world at bottom after all, in spite of its pretenses and in spite of appearances! It cannot by a stretch of imagination conceive that anything exists, of which it has not cognizance in its own heart. It will not admit into its imagination the mere idea that we have faith, because it does not know what faith is from experience, and it will not admit that there is anything in the mind of man which it does not experience itself, for that would be all one with admitting that there is such a thing as a mystery. It must be the measure of all things, and so in self-defense it considers us hypocritical, as professing what we cannot believe, lest it should be forced to confess itself blind. "See what love the Father has given us, that we should be called children of God; and so we are. The reason why the world does not know us is that it did not know him" (1 Jn 3:1).

What thankfulness should be ours that God has brought us into the Church of his Son! What gift is equal to it in the whole world in its preciousness and in its rarity? To find ourselves where we can use every faculty of the mind and affection of the heart in its perfection, to find ourselves in the possession of certainty, consistency, stability, on the highest and holiest subjects of human thought, to have hope here and heaven hereafter, to be on the Mount with Christ, while the poor world is guessing and quarrelling at its foot: who among us shall not wonder at his own blessedness? Who shall not be awe-struck at the inscrutable grace of God, which has brought himself, not others, where he stands?

Monday of the Fourth Week of Lent

Bodily Suffering

Our Lord and Savior Jesus Christ came by blood as well as by water, not only as a fount of grace and truth—the source of spiritual light, joy, and salvation—but as a combatant with sin and Satan. He was consecrated through suffering. He was, in the words of the apostle, "clothed in a robe dipped in blood" (Rev 19:13). It was the untold sufferings of the Eternal Word in our nature, his body dislocated and torn, his blood poured out, his soul violently separated by a painful death, which has put away from us the wrath of him whose love sent him for that very purpose. This only was our atonement. No one shared in the work. He trod "the wine press alone, and from the peoples no one was with him" (see Is 63:3). When lifted up upon the cursed tree, he fought with all the hosts of evil and conquered by suffering.

Thus, in a most mysterious way, all that is needful for this sinful world, the life of our souls, the regeneration of our nature, all that is most joyful and glorious—hope, light, peace, spiritual freedom, holy influences, religious knowledge and strength—all flow from a fount of blood. A work of blood is our salvation; and we, if we would be saved, must draw near and gaze upon it in faith and accept it as the way to heaven. We must take him who thus suffered as our guide. We must embrace his sacred feet and follow him. No wonder, then, should we receive on ourselves some drops of his sacred agony which bedewed his garments. No wonder, should we be sprinkled with the sorrows which he bore in expiation of our sins.

And so it has ever been in very deed. To approach him has been, from the first, to be partaker, more or less, in his sufferings. Not in the case of every individual who believes in him, but as regards the more conspicuous, the more favored, his choice instruments, and his most active servants. That is, it has been the lot of the Church on the whole and of those who had been most like him as rulers, intercessors, and teachers of the Church. He, indeed, alone meritoriously; they, because they have been near him. Thus, immediately upon his birth, he brought the sword upon the infants of his own age at Bethlehem. His very shadow, cast upon a city where he did not abide, was stained with blood. His blessed Mother had not clasped him to her breast for many weeks before she was warned of the penalty of that fearful privilege: "a sword will pierce through your own soul also" (Lk 2:35). Virtue went out of him, but the water and the blood flowed together as afterwards from his pierced side. Most of his apostles passed through life-long sufferings to a violent death. In particular, when the favored brothers, James and John, came to him with a request that they might sit beside him in his kingdom, he plainly stated this connection between nearness to him and affliction. "Are you able," he said, "to drink the chalice that I am to drink?" (Mt 20:22). It was as if he had said, "You cannot have the sacraments of grace without the painful figures of them. The Cross, when imprinted on your foreheads, will draw blood. You shall receive, indeed, the baptism of the Spirit and the cup of my communion, but it shall be with the attendant pledges of my cup of agony and my baptism of blood." Elsewhere he speaks the same language to all who would partake the benefits of his death and passion: "Whoever does not bear his own cross and come after me, cannot be my disciple" (Lk 14:27).

Accordingly, his apostles frequently remind us of this necessary, though mysterious, appointment, and bid us not to be "surprised at the fiery ordeal which comes upon you to prove you, as though something strange were happening to you. But rejoice in so far as you share Christ's sufferings" (1 Pet 4:12-13). St. Paul teaches the same lesson when he speaks of taking up the remnant of Christ's sorrows as some precious mantle dropped from the Cross and wearing it for his sake. "I rejoice in my sufferings for your sake, and in my flesh I complete what is lacking in Christ's afflictions for the sake of his body, that is, the church" (Col 1:24). And though he is speaking especially of persecution and other sufferings borne in the cause of the Gospel, yet it is our great privilege, as Scripture tells us, that all pain and trouble borne in faith and patience will be accounted as marks of Christ, grace-tokens from the absent Savior, and will be accepted and rewarded for his sake at the last day. It declares generally, "When you pass through the waters I will be with you; and through the rivers, they shall not overwhelm you; when you walk through fire you shall not be burned, and the flame shall not consume you" (Is 43:2). "For this slight momentary affliction is preparing for us an eternal weight of glory beyond all comparison" (2 Cor 4:17).

Let us, then, determine with cheerful hearts to sacrifice unto the Lord our God our comforts and pleasures, however innocent, when he calls for them, whether for the purposes of his Church or in his own inscrutable Providence. Let us lend to him a few short hours of present ease, and we shall receive our own with abundant interest in the day of his coming. There is a treasury in heaven stored with such offerings as the natural man abhors, with sighs and tears, wounds and blood, torture and death. The martyrs first began the contribution, and we all may follow them. All of us, because every suffering, great or little, may, like the widow's mite, be sacrificed in faith to him who sent it. Christ gave us the words of consecration: "Thy will be done" (Mt 6:10). Henceforth, as the apostle speaks, we may "rejoice in our sufferings" (Rom 5:3) as the seed of future glory.

Meanwhile, let us never forget in all we suffer that, properly speaking, our own sin is the cause of it, and it is only by Christ's mercy that we are allowed to range ourselves at his side. We who are children of wrath are made through him children of grace, and our pains—which are in themselves but the foretastes of hell—are changed by the sprinkling of his blood into a preparation for heaven.

Tuesday of the Fourth Week of Lent

Scripture a Record of Human Sorrow

What a scene of misery the pool of Bethesda must have presented. There lay about it "a multitude of invalids, blind, lame, paralyzed" (Jn 5:3). This is a painful picture, such as we do not like to dwell upon. It is a picture of a chief kind of human suffering, bodily disease, one which suggests to us and typifies all other suffering, the most obvious fulfillment of that curse which Adam's fall brought upon his descendants. Now, it must strike everyone who thinks at all about it that the Bible is full of such descriptions of human misery. We know it also abounds in accounts of human sin, but not to speak of these, it abounds in accounts of human distress and suffering, of our miserable condition, of the vanity, unprofitableness, and trials of life.

The Bible begins with the history of the curse pronounced on the earth and man; it ends with the Book of Revelation, a portion of Scripture fearful for its threats and its prediction of judgments. And whether the original curse on Adam be now removed from the world or not, it is certain that God's awful curses, foretold by St. John, are on all sides of us. Surely, in spite of the peculiar promises made to the Church in Christ our Savior, yet as regards the world, the volume of inspiration is still a dreary record with "writing on the front and on the back, and there were written on it words of lamentation and mourning and woe" (Ez 2:10). And further, it seems to drop what might be said in favor of this life and enlarges on the unpleasant side of it. The history passes quickly from the Garden of Eden to dwell on the sufferings that followed when our first parents were expelled from it. And though, in matter of fact, there are traces of paradise still left among us, yet it is evident that Scripture says little of them in comparison with its accounts of human misery. Little does it say concerning the innocent pleasures of life, of those temporal blessings which rest upon our worldly occupations and make them easy, of the blessings which we derive from the succession of the seasons and the produce of the earth, little about our recreations and our daily domestic comforts, little about the ordinary occasions of festivity and mirth which occur in life. Human tales and poems are full of pleasant sights and prospects; they make things better than they are and portray a sort of imaginary perfection, but Scripture seems to abstain even from what might be said in praise of human life as it is. We read, indeed, of the feast made when Isaac was weaned, of Jacob's marriage, of the domestic and religious festivities of Job's family, but these are exceptions in the tenor of the Scripture history. "Vanity of vanities, all is vanity" (Eccles 1:1); "Man is born to trouble" (Job 5:7): these are its customary lessons.

So much is this the case that thoughtless persons are averse to the Scripture narrative for this very reason. Not bad men, but thoughtless persons, and of these there are many who consider the Bible a gloomy book and on that account seldom look into it, saying it makes them melancholy. Accordingly, there have been attempts made to hide this austere character of the Scripture and make it a bright interesting picture of human life. Its stories have before now been embellished in human language to suit the taste of weak and cowardly minds. All this shows that, in the common opinion of mankind, the Bible does not take a pleasant sunshine view of the world.

God does nothing without some wise and good reason, which it becomes us devoutly to accept and use. He has not given us this dark view of the world without a cause. In truth, this view is the ultimate true view of human life. But this is not all. It is a view which it concerns us much to know. It concerns us much to be told that this world is, after all, in spite of first appearances and partial exceptions, a dark world, else we shall be obliged to learn it—and sooner or later we must learn it—by sad experience, whereas, if we are forewarned, we shall unlearn false notions of its excellence and be saved the disappointment which follows them. And therefore it is that Scripture omits even what might be said in praise of this world's pleasures, not denying their value such as it is, nor forbidding us to use them religiously, but knowing that we are sure to find them out for ourselves without being told of them and that our danger is on the side, not of undervaluing, but of overvaluing them. Whereas, being told of the world's vanity at first, we shall learn not indeed to be gloomy and discontented, but to bear a sober and calm heart under a smiling cheerful countenance. This is one chief reason of the solemn character of the Scripture history, and if we keep it in view, far from being offended and frightened by its notes of sorrow, because they grate on the ear at first, we shall steadfastly listen to them and get them by heart as a gracious gift from God sent to us as a remedy for all dangerous overflowing joy, in order to save us far greater pain, the pain of actual disappointment, such as the overthrow of vainly cherished hopes of lasting good upon earth will certainly occasion.

Our Savior gave us a pattern which we are bound to follow. He was far greater than John the Baptist, yet he came not with St. John's outward austerity. He condemned the display of strictness or gloominess that we, his followers, might fast the more in private and be the more austere in our secret hearts. True it is that such self-command, composure, and inward faith are not learned in a day, but if they were, why should this life be given to us? It is given us as a very preparation time for obtaining them. Only look upon the world in this light: its sights of sorrows are to calm you and its pleasant sights to try you. There is a bravery in thus going straightforward, shrinking from no duty little or great, passing from high to low, from pleasure to pain, and making your principles strong without their becoming formal. Learn to be as the angel who could descend among the miseries of Bethesda without losing his heavenly purity or his perfect happiness. Gain healing from troubled waters. Make up your mind to the prospect of sustaining a certain measure of pain and trouble in your passage through life. By the blessing of God, this will prepare you for it. It will make you thoughtful and resigned without interfering with your cheerfulness. It will connect you in your own thoughts with the saints of Scripture, whose lot it was to be patterns of patient endurance, and this association brings to the mind a peculiar consolation. And read the Gospels, finding accounts of sick and afflicted persons and, above all, of Christ's sufferings, which are far more than enough to make the world, bright as it may be, look dark and miserable in itself to all true believers, even if the record of them were the only sorrowful part of the whole Bible.

Wednesday of the Fourth Week of Lent

Christ's Privations, a Meditation for Christians

What is meditating on Christ? It is simply this, thinking habitually and constantly of him and of his deeds and sufferings. It is to have him before our minds as one whom we may contemplate, worship, and address when we rise up, when we lie down, when we eat and drink, when we are at home and abroad, when we are working, or walking, or at rest, when we are alone, and again when we are in company: this is meditating. And by this, and nothing short of this, will our hearts come to feel as they ought. We have stony hearts, hearts as hard as highways; the history of Christ makes no impression on them. And yet, if we would be saved, we must have tender, sensitive, living hearts. Our hearts must be broken, must be broken up like ground, and dug, and watered, and tended, and cultivated, till they become as gardens acceptable to our God, gardens in which the Lord God may walk and dwell. The dry and barren waste must burst forth into springs of living water. This change must take place in our hearts if we would be saved; in a word, we must have what we have not by nature—faith and love—and how is this to be effected, under God's grace, but by godly and practical meditation through the day?

Come then, let us review some of the privations of the Son of God made man, which should be our meditation during these holy days.

He came in poverty. St. Paul said, "You know the grace of our Lord Jesus Christ, that though he was rich, yet for your sake he became poor, so that by his poverty you might become rich" (2 Cor 8:9). Let not the poor suppose that their hardships are their own only and that no one else ever felt them. The Most High God, God the Son, who had reigned with the Father from everlasting, supremely blessed, became a poor man and suffered the hardships of the poor. Where was he born? In a stable. What was his first cradle? A manger. He says on one occasion, "Foxes have holes, and birds of the air have nests; but the Son of man has nowhere to lay his head" (Lk 9:58). He had no home. He was, when he began to preach, what would now be called with contempt a vagrant. He was constantly journeying during his ministry, and journeying on foot. Once he rode into Jerusalem, to fulfill a prophecy.

Now let us proceed to other greater sufferings, which he took on himself when he became poor. Contempt, hatred, and persecution from the world was one of these. Even in his infancy, Mary had to flee with him into Egypt to hinder Herod from killing him. When he returned, it was not safe to dwell in Judea, and he was brought up in Nazareth, a place of evil name, where the holy Virgin had been when Gabriel came to her. He was set at naught and persecuted by the Pharisees and priests when he began to preach, and had again and again to flee for his life, which they were bent on taking.

But all these were but the beginning of sorrows with him. To see their fullness, we must look on his passion. In the anguish which he then endured, we see all his other sorrows concentrated and exceeded.

Observe, first, what is very wonderful and awful, the overwhelming fear he had of his sufferings before they came. This shows how great they were, but it would seem besides this, as if he had decreed to go through all trials for us, and, among them, the trial of fear. He says, "Now is my soul troubled. And what shall I say? 'Father, save me from this hour'? No, for this purpose I have come to this hour'" (Jn 12:27).

Next, he was betrayed to death by one of his own friends. What a bitter stroke is this! He was lonely enough without this, but in this last trial, one of the twelve apostles, his own familiar friend, betrayed him, and the others forsook him and fled, though St. Peter and St. John afterwards recovered heart a little and followed him. Yet soon St. Peter himself incurred a worse sin by denying him thrice. How affectionately he felt towards them, and how he drew towards them with a natural movement of heart upon the approach of his trial, though they disappointed him, is plain from the words he used towards them at his Last Supper: "I have earnestly desired to eat this passover with you before I suffer" (Lk 22:15).

Soon after this his sufferings began, and both in soul and in body was this holy and blessed Savior, the Son of God and Lord of life, given over to the malice of the great enemy of God and man. His head was crowned and torn with thorns and bruised with staves. His face was defiled with spitting. His shoulders were weighed down with the heavy cross. His back was rent and gashed with scourges. His hands and feet gored through with nails. His side, by way of insult, wounded with the spear. His mouth parched with intolerable thirst, and his soul so bedarkened that he cried out, "My God, my God, why have you forsaken me?" (Mt 27:46). And thus he hung upon the Cross. Surely to him alone, in their fullness, apply the prophet's words: "Look and see if there is any sorrow like my sorrow which was brought upon me, which the Lord inflicted on the day of his fierce anger" (Lam 1:12).

How little are our sorrows to these! How little is our pain, our hardships, our persecutions, compared with those which Christ voluntarily undertook for us! How base and miserable are we for understanding them so little, for being so little impressed by them! This holy season should be a time of mourning, as when a dead body is in a house. We cannot, indeed, thus feel, merely because we wish and ought so to feel. We cannot force ourselves into so feeling. We cannot work ourselves up into such feelings, or, if we can, it is better we should not, because it *is* a working up, which is bad. Deep feeling is but the natural and necessary attendant on a holy heart. But though we cannot at our will thus feel, and at once, we can go the way thus to feel. We can grow in grace till we thus feel. And, meanwhile, we can observe such an outward abstinence from the innocent pleasures and comforts of life as may prepare us for thus feeling, such an abstinence as we should spontaneously observe if we did thus feel. We may meditate upon Christ's sufferings, and by this meditation we shall gradually, as time goes on, be brought to these deep feelings. We may pray to God to do for us what we cannot do for ourselves, to make us feel, to give us the spirit of gratitude, love, reverence, self-abasement, godly fear, repentance, holiness, and lively faith.

Thursday of the Fourth Week of Lent

Miracles No Remedy for Unbelief

Nothing is more surprising than the history of God's chosen people. It seems strange, indeed, that the Israelites should have acted as they did, age after age, in spite of the miracles which were granted to them. The laws of nature were suspended again and again before their eyes. The most marvelous signs were wrought at the word of God's prophets, and for their deliverance, yet they did not obey their great benefactor at all better than men today who have not these advantages. Age after age, God visited them by angels, by inspired messengers; age after age, they sinned. At last he sent his well-beloved Son, and he wrought miracles before them still more abundant, wonderful, and beneficent than any had before. What was the effect upon them of his coming? St. John tells us, "the chief priests and the Pharisees gathered the council, and said, "What are we to do? For this man performs many signs . . . so from that day on they took counsel about how to put him to death" (Jn 11:47, 53).

In matter of fact, then, whatever be the reason, nothing is gained by miracles, nothing comes of miracles, as regards our religious views, principles, and habits. Hard as it is to believe, miracles certainly do not make men better: the history of Israel proves it.

Let us consider this startling truth.

Why should the sight of a miracle make you better than you are? Do you doubt at all the being and power of God? No. Do you doubt what you ought to do? No. Do you doubt at all that the rain, for instance, and sunshine come from him? Or that the fresh life of each year as it comes is his work, and that all nature bursts into beauty and richness at his bidding? You do not doubt it at all. Nor do you doubt that it is your duty to obey him who made the world and who made you. And yet, with the knowledge of all this, you find you cannot prevail upon yourselves to do what you know you should do. Knowledge is not what you want to make you obedient. You have knowledge enough already. Now what truth would a miracle convey to you which you do not learn from the works of God around you? What would it teach you concerning God which you do not already believe without having seen it?

But, you will say, a miracle would startle you. True. But would not the startling pass away? Could you be startled forever? And what sort of religion is that which consists in a state of fright and disturbance? Are you not continually startled by the accidents of life? You see, you hear things suddenly, which bring before the mind the thought of God and judgment; calamities befall you which for the time sober you. Startling is not conversion, any more than knowledge is practice.

But you urge that perhaps that startling might issue in amendment of life, that it might be the beginning of a new course, though it passed away itself, that a miracle would not indeed convert you, but it would be the first step towards a conversion, that it would be the turning point in your life. It is very true that sudden emotions—fear, hope, gratitude, and the like—do produce such effects sometimes. But why is a miracle necessary to produce such effects? Other things startle us besides miracles; we have a number of accidents sent to us by God to startle us. He has not left us without warnings, though he has not given us miracles. And if we are not moved and converted by those which come upon us, the probability is that, like the Jews, we should not be converted by miracles.

Let us then put aside vain excuses, and, instead of looking for outward events to change our course of life, be sure of this, that if our course of life is to be changed, it must be from within. God's grace moves us from within, so does our own will. External circumstances have no real power over us. If we do not love God, it is because we have not wished to love him, tried to love him, prayed to love him. We have not borne the idea and the wish in our mind day by day. We have not had it before us in the little matters of the day. We have not lamented that we loved him not. We have been too indolent, sluggish, carnal, to attempt to love him in little things and begin at the beginning. We have shrunk from the effort of moving from within. We have been like persons who cannot get themselves to rise in the morning. And we have desired and waited for a thing impossible: to be changed once and for all, all at once, by some great excitement from without, or some great event, or some special season. Something or other we go on expecting, which is to change us without our having the trouble to change ourselves. We covet some miraculous warning, or we complain that we are not in happier circumstances, that we have so many cares, or so few religious privileges. Or we look forward for a time when religion will come easy to us as a matter of course.

Let us rouse ourselves and act as reasonable men before it is too late. Let us understand, as a first truth in religion, that *love* of heaven is the only *way* to heaven. Sight will not move us, else why did Judas persist in covetousness in the very presence of Christ? Why did Satan fall, when he was a bright archangel? Nor will reason subdue us, else why was the Gospel, in the beginning, "folly to gentiles"? (1 Cor 1:23). Nor will excited feelings convert us, for there are those who "when they hear the word, receive it with joy," but having no root, "believe for a while and in time of temptation fall away" (Lk 8:13). Nor will self-interest prevail with us, or the rich man whose land "brought forth plentifully" would have been more prudent and would have recollected that this night his soul might be required of him (Lk 12:16-20). Let us understand that nothing but the love of God can make us believe in him or obey him, and let us pray to him who has prepared for them that love him such good things as pass man's understanding to pour into our hearts such love towards him that we, loving him above all things, may obtain his promises, which exceed all that we can desire.

Friday of the Fourth Week of Lent

The Good Portion of Mary

Martha and Mary were sisters of Lazarus, who was afterwards raised from the dead. All three lived together, but Martha was mistress of the house. St. Luke mentions that Christ came to a certain village, "and a woman named Martha received him into her house" (Lk 10:38). Being then at the head of a family, she had duties which necessarily engaged her time and thoughts. And on the present occasion she was especially busy, from a wish to do honor to the Lord. "Martha was distracted with much serving" (Lk 10:40). Her sister was free from the necessity of worldly business by being the younger. "She had a sister called Mary, who sat at the Lord's feet and listened to his teaching" (Lk 10:39). The same distinction, at once of duty and character, appears in the narrative of Lazarus' death and restoration, as contained in St. John's Gospel. "When Martha heard that Jesus was coming, she went and met him, while Mary sat in the house" (Jn 11:20). Afterwards, Martha "went and called her sister Mary, saying quietly, 'The Teacher is here and is calling for you'" (Jn 11:28). Again, in the beginning of the following chapter, "they made him a supper; Martha served, and . . . Mary took a pound of costly ointment of pure nard and anointed the feet of Jesus and wiped his feet with her hair" (Jn 12:2-3). In these passages the same general difference between the sisters presents itself, though in a different respect. Martha still directs and acts, while Mary is the retired and modest servant of Christ, who, at liberty from worldly duties, loves to sit at his feet and hear his voice, and silently honors him with her best, without obtruding herself upon his sacred presence.

To return, "Martha was distracted with much serving; and she went to him and said, "Lord, do you not care that my sister has left me to serve alone? Tell her then to help me" (Lk 10:40). And Jesus "answered her, 'Martha, Martha, you are anxious and troubled about many things; one thing is needful. Mary has chosen the good portion, which shall not be taken away from her'" (Lk 10:41-42).

Mary's portion is the better of the two. Our Lord does not expressly say it, but he clearly implies it. If his words be taken literally, they might even mean that Martha's heart was not right with him, which, it is plain from other parts of the history, they do not mean. Therefore, what he intimated surely was that Martha's portion was full of snares, as being one of worldly labor, but that Mary could not easily go wrong in hers, that we may be busy in a wrong way, we cannot well adore him except in a right one, that to serve God by prayer and praise continually, when we can do so consistently with other duties, is the pursuit of the one thing needful and the good portion which shall not be taken away.

It is impossible to read St. Paul's epistles carefully without perceiving how faithfully they comment on this rule of our Lord's. They speak much and often of the duties of worship, meditation, thanksgiving, prayer, praise, and intercession, and in such a way as to lead the Christian, so far as other duties will allow him, to make them the ordinary employment of his life, not, indeed, to neglect his lawful calling, nor even to be content without some active efforts to do good, yet to devote himself to a life at Jesus' feet and a continual hearing of his word.

Consider the following passages as illustrations of that more blessed portion with which Mary was favored. "Continue steadfastly in prayer, being watchful in it with thanksgiving" (Col 4:2). "Let the word of Christ dwell in you richly, as you teach and admonish one another in all wisdom, and as you sing psalms and hymns and spiritual songs with thankfulness in your hearts to God" (Col 3:16). "Do not get drunk with wine, for that is debauchery; but be filled with the Spirit, addressing one another in psalms and hymns and spiritual songs, singing and making melody to the Lord with all your heart, always and for everything giving thanks in the name of our Lord Jesus Christ to God the Father" (Eph 5:18-20). "Pray at all times in the Spirit, with all prayer and supplication. To that end keep alert with all perseverance, making supplication for all the saints" (Eph 6:18). Thus St. Paul speaks, and in like manner St. Peter: "cast all your anxieties on him, for he cares about you" (1 Pet 5:7). "The end of all things is at hand; therefore keep sane and sober for your prayers" (1 Pet 4:7). And also St. James, "Is any one among you suffering? Let him pray. Is any cheerful? Let him sing praise" (Jas 5:13).

From that time onward to the present day, Mary's lot has been offered to vast multitudes of Christians, if they could receive it. Blessed indeed are they whom Christ calls near to him to be his own peculiar attendants and familiar friends. Blessed even if they are allowed to seize intervals of such service towards him, but favored and honored beyond thought if they can, without breach of duty, put aside worldly things with full purpose of heart and present themselves as a holy offering, without spot or blemish, to him who died for them. These are they who "follow the Lamb wherever he goes" (Rev 14:4), and to them he more especially addresses those lessons of faith and resignation which are recorded in his Gospel. "Do not be anxious about your life, what you shall eat, nor about your body, what you shall put on. . . . Consider the lilies, how they grow; they neither toil nor spin;

yet I tell you, even Solomon in all his glory was not clothed like one of these. But if God so clothes the grass which is alive in the field today and tomorrow is thrown into the oven, how much more will he clothe you, O men of little faith! And do not seek what you are to eat and what you are to drink, nor be of anxious mind. For all the nations of the world seek these things; and your Father knows that you need them. Instead, seek his kingdom, and these things shall be yours as well" (Lk 12:22-31).

Saturday of the Fourth Week of Lent

God's Will the End of Life

Why were you sent into the world? It is perhaps a thought more obvious than it is common. It ought to come into your minds, but it does not. There are those who recollect the first time when it came home to them. They were but little children, and they were by themselves, and they spontaneously asked themselves, or rather God spoke in them, "Why am I here? How came I here? Who brought me here? What am I to do here?" Perhaps it was the first act of reason, the beginning of their real responsibility, the commencement of their trial. Perhaps from that day they may date their capacity, their awful power, of choosing between good and evil, and of committing mortal sin. And so, as life goes on, the thought comes vividly, from time to time, for a short season across their conscience, whether in illness, or in some anxiety, or at some season of solitude, or on hearing some preacher, or reading some religious work. A vivid feeling comes over them of the vanity and unprofitableness of the world, and then the question recurs, "Why then am I sent into it?"

A great contrast indeed does this vain, unprofitable, yet overbearing world present with such a question as that. The world professes to supply all that we need, as if we were sent into it for the sake of being sent here, and for nothing beyond the sending. Every man is doing his own will here, seeking his own pleasure, pursuing his own ends, and that is why he was brought into existence. Go abroad into the streets of the populous city, contemplate the continuous outpouring there of human energy, and the countless varieties of human character, and be satisfied! The streets are lined with shops, inviting customers, and widen now and then into some spacious square or place, with lofty masses of brickwork or of stone, gleaming in the fitful sunbeam, and surrounded or fronted with what simulates a garden's foliage. Oh, this curious, restless, clamorous, panting being, which we call life! And is there to be no end to all this? Is there no object in it? It never has an end; it is its own object! Is it not a shocking thought? But who can deny the truth that the multitude of men are living without any aim beyond this visible scene.

What a contrast is all this to the end of life as it is set before us in our most holy Faith. If there was one among the sons of men who might allowably have taken his pleasure and have done his own will here below, surely it was he who came down on earth from the bosom of the Father, and who was so pure and spotless in that human nature which he put on him that he could have no human purpose or aim inconsistent with the will of his Father. Yet he, the Son of God, the Eternal Word, came, not to do his own will, but his who sent him.

Hence it is that he was carried in the womb of a poor woman, who, before his birth, had two journeys to make, of love and of obedience, to the mountains and to Bethlehem. He was born in a stable and laid in a manger. He was hurried off to Egypt to sojourn there. Then he lived till he was thirty years of age in a poor way, by a rough trade, in a small house, in a despised town. Then, when he went out to preach, he had not where to lay his head. He wandered up and down the country, as a stranger upon earth. He was driven out into the wilderness and dwelt among the wild beasts. He endured heat and cold, hunger and weariness, reproach and calumny. His food was coarse bread, and fish from the lake, or depended on the hospitality of strangers. And as he had already left his Father's greatness on high and had chosen an earthly home, so again, at that Father's bidding, he gave up the sole solace given him in this world and denied himself his mother's presence. He endured to call her coldly "woman" (Jn 2:4), who was his own undefiled one, all beautiful, all gracious, the best creature of his hands and the sweet nurse of his infancy. He exemplified in his own person the severe maxim, "he who loves father or mother more than me is not worthy of me" (Mt 10:37). In all these many ways, he sacrificed every wish of his own, that we might understand, that, if he, the Creator, came into his own world, not for his own pleasure, but to do his Father's will, we too have most surely some work to do, and have seriously to consider what that work is.

Yes, so it is. Everyone who breathes, high and low, educated and ignorant, young and old, man and woman, has a mission, has a work. We are not sent into this world for nothing. We are not born at random. We are not here that we may go to bed at night, and get up in the morning, toil for our bread, eat and drink, laugh and joke, sin when we have a mind, and reform when we are tired of sinning, rear a family and die. God sees every one of us. He creates every soul. He needs, he deigns to need, every one of us. He has an end for each of us. We are placed in our different ranks and stations, not to get what we can out of them for ourselves but to labor in them for him. As Christ has his work, we too have ours. As he rejoiced to do his work, we must rejoice in ours also.

The simple question is, whatever a man's rank in life may be, does he in that rank perform the work which God has given him to do?

The end of a thing is the test. It was our Lord's rejoicing in his last solemn hour, that he had done the work for which he was sent. "I glorified you on earth," he says in his prayer, "having accomplished the work which you gave me to do . . . I have manifested your name to the men whom you gave me out of the world" (Jn 17:4-6). It was St. Paul's consolation also: "I have fought the good fight, I have finished the race, I have kept the faith" (2 Tim 4:7). Alas! how different will be our view of things when we come to die, or when we have passed into eternity, from the dreams and pretenses with which we beguile ourselves now! What will Babel do for us then? Will it rescue our souls from the purgatory or the hell to which it sends them? If we were created, it was that we might serve God. If we have his gifts, it is that we may glorify him. If we have a conscience, it is that we may obey it. If we have the prospect of heaven, it is that we may keep it before us. If we have light, that we may follow it. If we have grace, that we may save ourselves by means of it. Alas! for those who were called to be holy and lived in sin! Alas for those who have had gifts and talent, and have not used, or have misused, or abused them!

Sunday of the Fifth Week of Lent

The Tears of Christ, I

Why did our Lord weep at the grave of Lazarus? He knew he had power to raise him. Why should he act the part of those who sorrow for the dead? The whole narrative exhibits our Savior's conduct in various lights, which it is difficult for weak creatures, such as we are, properly to blend together.

When he first received the news of Lazarus's illness, "He stayed two days longer in the same place where he was." Then telling his disciples that Lazarus was dead, he said, "for your sake I am glad that I was not there," and that he would "go to awake him out of sleep." Then, when he was come to Bethany, where Lazarus dwelt, he saw the sorrow of the Jews and was "deeply moved in spirit and troubled." Lastly, in spite of his perturbation and weeping, he raised Lazarus (see Jn 11:6-44).

It is remarkable that such difficulties as these should lie on the face of Scripture, quite independently of those arising from the comparison of the texts in question with the doctrine of his divine nature. We know, indeed, there are insuperable mysteries involved in the union of his divine with his human attributes, which seem incompatible with each other; for instance, how he should be ever-blessed, and yet weep, all-knowing, yet apparently ignorant. Yet without entering into the consideration of the mysteries of faith, commonly so called, it is worth inquiring whether the very surface of the sacred history does not contain seeming inconsistencies of a nature to prepare us for such other difficulties as may lie from a deeper comparison of history with doctrine.

There is quite enough in the narrative to show that he who speaks is not one whose thoughts it is easy to get possession of; that it is no light matter to put oneself, even in part, into the position of his mind and to state under what feelings and motives he said this or that. In a word, it should be impressed upon us that our Savior's words are not of a nature to be heard once and no more, but that to understand them we must feed upon them, and live in them, as if by little and little growing into their meaning.

It would be well if we understood the necessity of this more than we do. It is very much the fashion at present to regard the Savior of the world in an irreverent and unreal way, as a mere idea or vision; to speak of him so narrowly and unfruitfully, as if we only knew of his name, though Scripture has set him before us in his actual sojourn on earth, in his gestures, words, and deeds, in order that we may have that on which to fix our eyes. And till we learn to do this, to leave off vague statements about his love, his willingness to receive the sinner, his imparting repentance and spiritual aid, and the like, and view him in his particular and actual works set before us in Scripture, surely we have not derived from the Gospels that very benefit which they are intended to convey. Nay, we are in some danger, perhaps, even as regards our faith; for, it is to be feared, while the thought of Christ is but a creation of our minds, it may gradually be changed or fade away, it may become defective or perverted; whereas, when we contemplate Christ as manifested in the Gospels, the Christ who exists therein, external to our own imaginings, and who is as really a living being, and sojourned on earth as truly as any of us, then we shall at length believe in him with a conviction, a confidence, and an entireness, which can no more be annihilated than the belief in our senses. It is impossible for a Christian mind to meditate on the Gospels, without feeling beyond all manner of doubt that he who is the subject of them is God; but it is very possible to speak in a vague way of his love towards us, and to use the name of Christ, yet not at all to realize that he is the Living Son of the Father, or to have any anchor for our faith within us, so as to be fortified against the risk of future defection.

What led our Lord to weep over the dead, who could at a word restore him, nay, had it in purpose so to do?

He wept from very sympathy with the grief of others. When Jesus saw Mary weeping, "and the Jews who came with her also weeping, he was deeply moved in spirit and troubled" (Jn 11:33). It is the very nature of compassion or sympathy, as the word implies, to "rejoice with those who rejoice, weep with those who weep" (Rom 12:15). We know it is so with men; and God tells us he also is compassionate, and full of tender mercy. Yet we do not well know what this means, for how can God rejoice or grieve? By the very perfection of his nature Almighty God cannot show sympathy, at least to the comprehension of beings of such limited minds as ours. He, indeed, is hid from us; but if we were allowed to see him, how could we discern in the Eternal and Unchangeable signs of sympathy? Words and works of sympathy he does display to us; but it is the very sight of sympathy in another that affects and comforts the sufferer more even than the fruits of it. Now we cannot see God's sympathy; and the Son of God, though feeling for us as great compassion as his Father, did not show it to us while he remained in his Father's bosom. But when he took flesh and appeared on earth, he showed us the Godhead in a new manifestation. He invested himself with a new set of attributes, those of our flesh, taking into him a human soul and body, in order that thoughts, feelings, affections might be his, which could respond to ours and certify to us his tender mercy. When, then, our Savior weeps from sympathy at Mary's tears, let us not say it is the love of a man overcome by natural feeling. It is the love of God, the bowels of compassion of the Almighty and Eternal, condescending to show it as we are capable of receiving it, in the form of human nature.

Jesus wept not merely from the deep thoughts of his understanding but from spontaneous tenderness, from the gentleness and mercy, the encompassing loving-kindness and exuberant affection of the Son of God for his own work, the race of man. Their tears touched him at once, as their miseries had brought him down from heaven. His ear was open to them, and the sound of their weeping went at once to his heart.

Monday of the Fifth Week of Lent

The Tears of Christ, II

Christ's pity, spontaneously excited by the sorrow of his friends, was awakened and began to look around upon the miseries of the world. What was it he saw? He saw visibly displayed the victory of death, a mourning multitude, everything present which might waken sorrow except him who was the chief object of it. He was not; a stone marked the place where he lay. Martha and Mary, whom he had known and loved in their brother's company, now solitary, approached him, first one and then the other, in far other mood and circumstance than heretofore—in deep affliction, in faith indeed and resignation, yet, apparently, with somewhat of a tender complaint: "Lord, if you had been here, my brother would not have died" (Jn 11:21, 32). Such has been the judgment passed, or the doubt raised, concerning him, in the breast of the creature in every age. Men have seen sin and misery around them, and, whether in faith or unbelief, have said, "If you had been here," if you had interfered, it might have been otherwise. Here, then, was the Creator surrounded by the works of his hands, who adored him indeed, yet seemed to ask why he suffered what he himself had made so to be marred. He would not tell them why it was. He chose another course for taking away their doubts and complaints. "He opened not his mouth" (Is 53:7), but he wrought wondrously. What he has done for all believers, revealing his atoning death yet not explaining it, this he did for Martha and Mary also, proceeding to the grave in silence to raise their brother while they complained that he had been allowed to die.

Christ was come to do a deed of mercy, and it was a secret in his own breast. He was conscious to himself that he loved him; but none could tell but he how earnest that affection was. Was he not in Joseph's case, who not in grief, but from the very fullness of his soul, and his desolateness in a heathen land, when his brethren stood before him, "turned away from them and wept" (Gen 42:24), as if his own tears were his best companions and had in them a sympathy to soothe that pain which none could share? Was Christ not in the case of a parent hanging over an infant and weeping upon it, from the very thought of its helplessness and insensibility to the love poured out upon it? But the parent weeps from the feeling of her weakness to defend it, knowing that what is now a child must grow up and take its own course, and (whether for earthly or heavenly good) must depend, not on her, but on the Creator and on itself. Christ's was a different contemplation, yet attended with its own peculiar emotion, the feeling that he had power to raise up Lazarus. Joseph wept, as having a secret, not only of the past, but of the future, of good in store as well as of evil done, of good which it was in his own power to confer. And our Lord and Savior knew that, while all seemed so dreary and hopeless, in spite of the tears and laments of his friends, in spite of the corpse four days old, he had the power which could overcome death, and he was about to use it. Is there any time more affecting than when you are about to break good news to a friend who has been stricken down by tidings of ill?

Alas, there were other thoughts still to call forth his tears. This marvelous benefit to the forlorn sisters, how was it to be attained? At his own cost. Christ was bringing life to the dead by his own death. His disciples would have dissuaded him from going into Judea, lest the Jews should kill him. Their apprehension was fulfilled. He went to raise Lazarus, and the fame of that miracle was the immediate cause of his seizure and crucifixion. This he knew beforehand. He saw Lazarus raised, the supper in Martha's house, Lazarus sitting at table with joy on all sides of him, Mary honoring her Lord on this festive occasion by the outpouring of the very costly ointment upon his feet, the Jews crowding not only to see him, but Lazarus also, his triumphant entry into Jerusalem, the multitude shouting Hosanna, the people testifying to the raising of Lazarus, the Greeks, who had come up to worship at the feast, earnest to see him, the children joining in the general joy, and then the Pharisees plotting against him, Judas betraying him, his friends deserting him, and the Cross receiving him. These things doubtless, among a multitude of thoughts unspeakable, passed over his mind. He felt that Lazarus was wakening to life at his own sacrifice, that he was descending into the grave which Lazarus left. He felt that Lazarus was to live and he to die; the appearance of things was to be reversed. The feast was to be kept in Martha's house, but the last passover of sorrow remained for him. He had come down from his Father's bosom to be an atonement of blood for all sin, and thereby to raise all believers from the grave, as he was then about to raise Lazarus; and to raise them, not for a time, but for eternity. And now the sharp trial lay before him, through which he was to open the kingdom of heaven to all believers. Contemplating then the fullness of his purpose while now going about a single act of mercy, he said to Martha, "I am the resurrection and the life; he who believes in me, though he die, yet shall he live, and whoever lives and believes in me shall never die" (Jn 11:25-26).

Wherever faith in Christ is, there is Christ himself. He said to Martha, "Do you believe this?" Wherever there is a heart to answer, "Yes, Lord, I believe" (Jn 11:26-27), there Christ is present. Blessed be his name! Nothing can rob us of this consolation: we will be as certain, through his grace, that he is standing over us in love, as though we saw him. We will not, after our experience of Lazarus's history, doubt an instant that he is thoughtful about us. He knows the beginnings of our illness, though he keeps at a distance. He knows when to remain away and when to draw near. He notes down the advances of it and the stages. He tells truly when his friend Lazarus is sick and when he sleeps. We all have experience of this and henceforth will never complain at the course of his providence. Only, we will beg of him an increase of faith, a more lively perception of the curse under which the world lies, and of our own personal demerits, a more understanding view of the mystery of his cross, a more devout and implicit reliance on the virtue of it, and a more confident persuasion that he will never put upon us more than we can bear, never afflict his brethren with any woe except for their own highest benefit.

Tuesday of the Fifth Week of Lent

Profession without Practice

Hypocrisy is a serious word. We are accustomed to consider the hypocrite as a hateful, despicable character, and an uncommon one. How is it, then, that our Blessed Lord, when surrounded by an innumerable multitude, began first of all to warn his disciples against hypocrisy, as though they were in special danger of becoming like those base deceivers, the Pharisees? "When so many thousands of the multitude had gathered together that they trod upon one another, he began to say to his disciples first, 'Beware of the leaven of the Pharisees, which is hypocrisy'" (Lk 12:1).

Our Lord's warning to us is to beware the leaven of the Pharisees, hypocrisy, which is professing without practicing. He warns us against it as a leaven, as a subtle insinuating evil which will silently spread itself throughout the whole character if we allow it. He warns us, lovingly considerate of us, lest we make ourselves a scorn and derision to the profane multitude who throng around to gaze curiously, or malevolently, or selfishly at his doings. They seek him, not as adoring him for his miracles' sake, but so that they can obtain something from him or can please their natural tastes while they profess to honor him. And in time of trial they desert him. They make a gain of godliness, or a fashion. So, he speaks not to them but to us, to his little flock, the Church, to whom it has been his Father's good pleasure to give the kingdom, and he bids us take heed of falling, as the Pharisees did before us, and like them coming short of our reward. He warns us that the pretense of religion never deceives beyond a little time, that sooner or later, "whatever you have said in the dark shall be heard in the light, and what you have whispered in private rooms shall be proclaimed upon the housetops" (Lk 12:3). Even in this world the discovery is often made. A man is brought into temptation of some sort or other and having no root in himself falls away and gives occasion to the enemies of the Lord to blaspheme. This will happen to him without himself being aware of it, for though a man begins to deceive others before he deceives himself, yet he does not deceive them for as long as he deceives himself. Their eyes are at length opened to him, while his own continue closed to himself. The world sees through him, detects, and triumphs in detecting his low motives and secular plans, while he is but very faintly sensible of them himself, much less has a notion that others clearly see them. And thus he will go on professing the highest principles and feelings, while bad men scorn him and insult true religion in his person.

This is the scandal which a Christian's inconsistency brings upon his cause, and it is not the fault of one or two men. The Christian world, so called, what is it practically but a witness for Satan rather than a witness for Christ? Rightly understood, doubtless the very disobedience of Christians witnesses for him who will overcome whenever he is judged. But is there any antecedent prejudice against religion so great as that which is occasioned by the lives of its professors? Let us ever remember that all who follow God with a half heart strengthen the hands of his enemies, give cause of exultation to wicked men, perplex inquirers after truth, and bring reproach upon their Savior's name. It is a known fact that unbelievers triumphantly maintain that the greater part of the English people is on their side, that the disobedience of professing Christians is a proof that whatever they say in their hearts they are unbelievers too. This we ourselves have perhaps heard said, and said not in the heat of argument or as satire, but in sober earnestness, from real and full persuasion that it is true. Men who have cast off their Savior console themselves with the idea that their neighbors, though too timid or too indolent openly to do so, yet in their real character do the same. And witnessing this general inconsistency, they despise them as unmanly, cowardly, and slavish, and hate religion as the origin of this debasement of mind.

"The people who in this country call themselves Christians," one of them might say, "with few exceptions are not believers, and every man of sense, whose bigotry has not blinded him, must see that persons who are evidently devoted to worldly gain, or worldly vanities, or luxurious enjoyments, though still preserving a little decency, while they pretend to believe the infinitely momentous doctrines of Christianity are performers in a miserable farce which is beneath contempt."

Such would be the words of an open enemy of Christ. The argument will not endure the trial of God's judgment at the last day, for no one is an unbeliever but by his own fault. But though no excuse for unbelievers, it is the condemnation of half-hearted Christians. What, indeed, will they plead before the throne of God when, on the revelation of all hidden deeds, the reviler of religion attributes his unbelief in a measure to the sight of their inconsistent conduct? When he mentions this action or that conversation, this violent or worldly conduct, that covetous or unjust transaction, or that self-indulgent life as partly the occasion of his falling away? "Woe to the world for temptations to sin! For it is necessary that temptations come, but woe to the man by whom the temptation comes" (Mt 18:7). Woe unto the deceiver and self-deceived. "The hope of the godless man shall perish. His confidence breaks in sunder, and his trust is a spider's web. He leans against his house, but it does not stand; he lays hold of it, but it does not endure" (Job 8:13-15). God give us grace to flee from this woe while we have time! Let us examine ourselves to see if there be any wicked way in us. Let us aim at obtaining some comfortable assurance that we are in the narrow way that leads to life. And let us pray God to enlighten us, to guide us, and to give us the will to please him, and the power.

Wednesday of the Fifth Week of Lent

The Testimony of Conscience

"Our boast is this, the testimony of our conscience that we have behaved in the world, and still more toward you, with holiness and godly sincerity, not by earthly wisdom but by the grace of God" (2 Cor 1:12). In these words, the great apostle appeals that he had lived in simplicity and sincerity, with a single aim and an innocent heart, as one who was illuminated and guided by God's grace. The like appeal he makes on other occasions. When brought before the Jewish council he says, "Brethren, I have lived before God in all good conscience up to this day" (Acts 23:1). And in his second epistle to Timothy, he speaks of having served God from his forefathers "with a clear conscience" (2 Tim 1:3). He was given to know his own sincerity in such measure that he could humbly take pleasure in it and be comforted by it. And so also speaks St. John: "Beloved, if our hearts do not condemn us, we have confidence before God" (1 Jn 3:21). Such was the confidence, such the rejoicing of St. Paul and St. John: not that they could do anything acceptable to God by their unaided powers, but that by his grace they could so live as to enjoy a cheerful hope of his favor, both now and evermore.

The same feeling is frequently expressed in the Psalms: a consciousness of innocence and integrity, a satisfaction in it, an appeal to God concerning it, and a confidence in God's favor in consequence. "Vindicate me, O Lord," says David, "for I have walked in my integrity, and I have trusted in the Lord without wavering." He proceeds to beg of God to aid him in this self-knowledge: "Prove me, O Lord, and try me; test my heart and my mind," that is, lest he should be deceived in thinking himself what he was not. He next enumerates the special points in which God had enabled him to obey. "I do not sit with false men, nor do I consort with dissemblers; I hate the company of evildoers, and I will not sit with the wicked. . . . But as for me, I walk in my integrity; redeem me, and have mercy on me. My foot stands on level ground; in the great congregation I will bless the Lord" (Ps 26:1-5, 11-12). In this and other passages of the Psalms, two points are brought before us: that it is possible to be innocent and to have that sense of our innocence which makes us happy in the thought of God's eye being upon us. Let us then dwell on a truth of which apostles and prophets unite in assuring us.

It is a frequent account of the kings of Judah that they walked or did not walk with God with a "blameless heart" (see 2 Chron 25:2). A man serves with a blameless heart who serves God in all parts of his duty, and not here and there, but here and there and everywhere, not perfectly indeed as regards the quality of obedience, but perfectly as regards its extent, not completely but consistently. Such a man may appeal to God with the Psalmist and say, "Prove me, O Lord, and try me; test my heart and my mind" (Ps 26:2) with the humble trust that there is no department of his duty on which Almighty God can put his hand and say, "Here you are not with me," no part in which he does not set God before him and desire to please him and to be governed by him. And something like this seems to be St. James's meaning when he says, by way of contrast, "For whoever keeps the whole law but fails in one point has become guilty of all of it" (Jas 2:10).

Not more different is ice from the flowing stream is a half purpose from a whole one. "He makes his wind blow, and the waters flow" (Ps 147:18). So is it when God prevails on a heart to open itself to him and admit him wholly. There is a perceptible difference of feeling in a man when he really gives himself up to God, when he gets himself honestly to say, "I sacrifice to you this cherished wish, this desire, this weakness, this scheme, this opinion: make me what you would have me. I bargain for nothing; I make no terms. I will be what you will make me, and all that you will make me. Try me, O Lord, and seek the ground of my heart; prove me and examine my thoughts; search each dark recess with your own bright light and lead me in the way everlasting." What a difference is this! What a feeling of satisfaction is poured over the mind! What a sense that at length we are doing what we should do and approving ourselves to God our Savior! Such is the blessedness and reward of confession. "I said, 'I will confess my transgressions to the Lord'; then you forgave the guilt of my sin" (Ps 32:5). He who comes to God to tell before him sorrowfully all that he knows wrong in himself is thereby desiring and beginning what is right and holy; and he who comes to beg him to work in him all that is right and holy, does thereby implicitly condemn and repent of all that is wrong in him. And thus he is altogether innocent, for all his life is made up either of honest endeavor or of honest confession, exactness in doing or sorrow for not doing, of simplicity and sincerity, repentance being on the one side of it and obedience on the other. Such the power divinely granted in the Gospel to an honest purpose.

Let us then, since this is our privilege, attempt to share in St. Paul's sincerity, that we may share in his rejoicing. Let us endeavor to become friends of God and fellow-citizens with the saints, not by sinless purity, for we have it not, not in deeds of great price, for we have none to show, but in that which is the fruit of baptism within us, an honest purpose, an unreserved entire submission of ourselves to our Maker, Redeemer, and Judge. Let us beg him to aid us in our endeavor, and, as he has begun a good work in us, to perform it until the day of the Lord Jesus.

Thursday of the Fifth Week of Lent

Profession without Hypocrisy

It is surely most necessary to beware, as our Lord solemnly bids us, of the leaven of the Pharisees, which is hypocrisy. We may be infected by it even though we are not conscious of our insincerity, for they did not know they were hypocrites. Nor need we have any definite bad object plainly before us, for they had none, only the vague desire to be seen and honored by the world. So, it would seem that there are vast multitudes of Pharisaical hypocrites among baptized Christians, that is, men professing without practicing. Nay, so far we may be called hypocritical one and all, for no Christian on earth altogether lives up to his profession.

This is even the ground on which some say that it is wrong to baptize and call Christians those who have not yet shown themselves to be really such. Rather, they say, it is a great evil, for it is to become hypocrites. Nay, really humble, well-intentioned men feel this about themselves. They shrink from retaining the blessed titles and privileges which Christ gave them in infancy, as being unworthy of them, and they fear lest they are really hypocrites like the Pharisees. Now, the obvious answer to this mistaken view of religion is to say that on the showing of such reasoners, no one at all ought to be baptized in any case and called a Christian, for no one acts up to his baptismal profession. No one believes, worships, and obeys duly, the Father, Son, and Holy Spirit, whose servant he is made in baptism. And yet the Lord did say, "Go, make disciples of all nations, baptizing them" (see Mt 28:19), clearly showing us that a man may be fit subject for baptism though he does not in fact practice everything that he professes, and, therefore, that any fears we may have, lest men should be in some sense like the Pharisees, do not keep us from making them Christians.

It is true that we profess to be saints, to be guided by the highest principles and to be ruled by the Spirit of God. We have long ago promised to believe and obey. It is also true that we cannot do these things aright. Nay, even with God's help—such is our sinful weakness—still we fall short of our duty. Nevertheless, we must not cease to profess. We must not put off from us the wedding garment which Christ gave us in baptism. We may still rejoice in him without being hypocrites, that is, if we labor day by day to make that wedding garment our own, to fix it on us and so incorporate it with our very selves that death, which strips us of all things, may be unable to tear it from us, though as yet it be in great measure but an outward garb, covering our own nakedness.

Let us recall how great God's mercy is in thus allowing us to clothe ourselves in the glory of Christ from the first, even before we are worthy of it. There is nothing so distressing to a true Christian as to have to prove himself such to others, both as being conscious of his own numberless failings and from his dislike of display. Now Christ has anticipated the difficulties of his modesty. He does not allow such a one to speak for himself; he speaks for him. He introduces each of us to his brethren, not as we are in ourselves—fit to be despised and rejected on account of the temptations which are in our flesh—but as messengers of God, even of Christ Jesus. It is our happiness that we need bring nothing in proof of our fellowship with Christians beside our baptism. This is what a great many persons do not understand. They think that none are to be accounted fellow-Christians but those who evidence themselves to be such to their fallible understandings, and hence they encourage others who wish for their praise to practice all kinds of display as a seal of their regeneration. Who can tell the harm this does to the true modesty of the Christian spirit? Instead of using the words of the Church and speaking to God, men are led to use their own words and make man their judge and justifier. They think it necessary to tell out their secret feelings and to enlarge on what God has done to their own souls in particular. And thus making themselves really answerable for all the words they use, which are altogether their own, they do in this case become hypocrites. They do say more than they can in reality feel. Of course, a religious man will naturally, and unawares, out of the very fullness of his heart, show his deep feeling and his conscientiousness to his near friends. But when to do so is made a matter of necessity, an object to be aimed at, and is an intentional act, then it is that hypocrisy must, more or less, sully our faith. "As many of you as were baptized into Christ have put on Christ," this is the apostle's decision (Gal 3:27). "There is neither Jew nor Greek, there is neither slave nor free, there is neither male nor female; for you are all one in Christ Jesus" (Gal 3:28). The Church follows this rule, and bidding us keep quiet, speaks for us, robes us from head to foot in the garments of righteousness, and exhorts us to live henceforth to God. But the disputer of this world reverses this procedure. He strips off all our privileges, tells us we must each be a Church to himself and must show himself to the world to be by himself and in himself the elect of God in order to prove his right to the privileges of a Christian.

Let us acknowledge all to be Christians who have not by open word or deed renounced their fellowship with us, and let us try to lead them on into all truth. And for ourselves, let us endeavor to enter more and more fully into the meaning of our own prayers and professions. Let us humble ourselves for the very little we do and the poor advance we make. Let us avoid unnecessary display of religion. Let us do our duty in that state of life to which God has called us. Thus proceeding, we shall, through God's grace, form within us the glorious mind of Christ. Whether rich or poor, learned or unlearned, walking by this rule, we shall become, at length, true saints, sons of God. We shall be upright and perfect, lights in the world, the image of him who died that we might be conformed to his likeness.

Friday of the Fifth Week of Lent

Religion a Weariness to the Natural Man

Religion is a weariness: such is the judgment commonly passed, often avowed, concerning the greatest of blessings which Almighty God has bestowed upon us. And when God gave the blessing, he at the same time foretold that such would be the judgment of the world upon it, even as manifested in the gracious person of him whom he sent to give it to us. "He had no form or comeliness," says the prophet, speaking of our Lord and Savior, "that we should look at him, and no beauty that we should desire him" (Is 53:2). He declared beforehand that to man his religion would be uninteresting and distasteful.

Not that this prediction excuses our deadness to it; this dislike of the religion given us by God himself, seen as it is on all sides of us—of religion in all its parts, whether its doctrines, its precepts, its polity, its worship, its social influence—this distaste for its very name, must obviously be an insult to its giver. But let us view it, as far as we dare, merely as a matter of fact and form a judgment on the probable consequences of it. Let us impress upon ourselves the fact of this contrariety between ourselves and our Maker: he having one will, we another; he declaring one thing to be good for us, and we fancying other objects to be our good.

Can we doubt that man's will runs contrary to God's will, that the view which the inspired word takes of our present life and of our destiny does not satisfy us as it rightly ought to do? That Christ has no form or comeliness in our eyes, and though we see him, we see no desirable beauty in him? That holy, merciful, and meek Savior, the Eternal, the only-Begotten Son of God, our friend and infinite benefactor, he who left the glory of his Father and died for us, who has promised us the overflowing riches of his grace both here and hereafter: he is a light shining in a dark place "and the darkness has not overcome it" (Jn 1:5). "Light has come into the world, and men loved darkness rather than light" (Jn 3:19). The nature of man is flesh, and that which is born of the flesh is flesh and ever must so remain. It never can discern, love, accept, the holy doctrines of the Gospel. It will occupy itself in various ways; it will take interest in things of sense and time, but it never can be religious. It is at enmity with God.

And now we see what must at once follow from what has been said. If our hearts are by nature set on the world for its own sake, and the world is one day to pass away, what are they to be set on, what to delight in then? Say, how will the soul feel when, stripped of its present attire, which the world bestows, it stands naked and shuddering before the pure, tranquil, and severe majesty of the Lord its God, its most merciful, yet dishonored Maker and Savior? What are to be the pleasures of the soul in another life? Can they be the same as they are here? They cannot. Scripture tells us they cannot. This world is passing away. Now what is there left to love and enjoy through a long eternity? What a dark, forlorn, miserable eternity that will be.

It is then plain enough, though Scripture said not a word on the subject, that if we would be happy in the world to come, we must make us new hearts and begin to love the things we naturally do not love. Viewing it as a practical point, the end of the whole matter is this: we must be changed. For we cannot expect the system of the universe to come over to us. The inhabitants of heaven, the numberless creations of angels, the glorious company of apostles, the goodly fellowship of the prophets, the noble army of martyrs, the holy Church universal, the will and attributes of God: these are fixed. We must go over to them. In our Savior's own authoritative words: "Truly, truly, I say to you, unless one is born anew, he cannot see the kingdom of God" (Jn 3:3). It is a plain matter of self-interest to turn our thoughts to the means of changing our hearts, putting out of the question our duty towards God and Christ, our Savior and Redeemer.

"He had no form or comeliness that we should look at him, and no beauty that we should desire him" (Is 53:2). It is not his loss that we love him not, it is our loss. He is all-blessed whatever becomes of us. He is not less blessed because we are far from him. It is we who are not blessed except as we approach him, except as we are like him, except as we love him. Woe unto us if in the day in which he comes from heaven we see nothing desirable or gracious in his wounds, but instead have made for ourselves an ideal blessedness, different from that which will be manifested to us in him. Woe unto us if we have made pride or selfishness or the carnal mind our standard of perfection and truth, if our eyes have grown dim and our hearts gross as regards the true light of men and the glory of the Eternal Father. May he himself save us from our self-delusions, whatever they are, and enable us to give up this world, that we may gain the next, and to rejoice in him who had no home of his own, no place to lay his head, who was poor and lowly and despised and rejected and tormented and slain.

Saturday of the Fifth Week of Lent

Endurance, the Christian's Portion

"All this has come upon me" (Gen 42:36). So spoke the Patriarch Jacob, when Joseph had been made away with, Simeon was detained in Egypt, Benjamin threatened, and his remaining sons suspected by him and distrusted, when at his door was a grievous famine, enemies or strangers round about, evil in prospect, and in the past a number of sad remembrances to pain, not to cheer him: the dreadful misconduct of his own family and its consequences, and, further back, the wrath of Esau, his separation from his father's house, his wanderings, and his ill-usage by Laban. From his youth upwards, he had been full of sorrows, and he bore them with a troubled mind. His first words are, "If God will be with me . . . then the Lord shall be my God" (Gen 28:20-21). His next, "All this has come upon me" (Gen 42:36). And his next, "few and evil have been the days of the years of my life" (Gen 47:9). Blow after blow, stroke after stroke, trouble came like hail. That one hailstone falls is a proof, not that no more will come, but that others are coming surely. Thus was it with Jacob. The storm muttered around him, and heavy drops fell while he was in his father's house; it drove him abroad. It did not therefore cease because he was out in it; it did not end because it had begun. Its beginning marked its presence. It began upon a law, which was extended over him in manhood also and old age, as in early youth. It was his calling to be in the storm. It was his very life to be a pilgrimage. It was the very thread of the days of his years to be few and evil.

In Jacob is prefigured the Christian. He said, "all this has
come upon me," and what he said in a sort of dejection of mind
that must the Christian say, not in dejection, not sorrowfully,
or passionately, or in complaint, or in impatience, but calmly,
as if confessing a doctrine. "All this has come upon me," but
it is my portion. They are against me, that I may fight against
them and overcome them. If there were no enemy, there could
be no conflict. Were there no trouble, there could be no faith.
Were there no trial, there could be no love. Were there no fear,
there could be no hope. Hope, faith, and love are weapons,
and weapons imply foes and encounters, and, relying on my
weapons, I will glory in my suffering, being "sure that neither
death, nor life, nor angels, nor principalities, nor things present,
nor things to come, nor powers, nor height, nor depth, nor
anything else in all creation, will be able to separate us from the
love of God in Christ Jesus our Lord" (Rom 8:38-39).

That trouble and sorrow are in some special sense the lot of
the Christian is plain from such passages of Scripture as when
St. Paul and St. Barnabas remind the disciples that "through
many tribulations we must enter the kingdom of God" (Acts
14:22), and when St. Peter says, "if when you do right and
suffer for it you take it patiently, you have God's approval" (1
Pet 2:20). It is objected, however, that times are changed since
the Gospel was first preached, and that what Scripture says
of the first Christians does not apply to us. We may answer
that while the Church maintains her ground, she ever suffers
in maintaining it. She has to fight the good fight in order to
maintain it. She fights, and she suffers in proportion as she plays
her part well, and if she is without suffering, it is because she is
slumbering. Her doctrines and precepts never can be palatable
to the world, and if the world does not persecute, it is because
the Church does not preach. And so of her individual members:

they in their own way suffer, not after her manner, perhaps, nor for the same reason, nor in the same degree, but more or less, as being under the law of suffering which Christ began. Judge not then by outward appearance. Think not that his servants are in ease and security because things look smooth, else you will be startled, perhaps, and offended when suffering falls upon you. Temporal blessings, indeed, he gives to you and to all men in abundance; "he makes his sun rise on the evil and on the good" (Mt 5:45). But in your case, it will be "houses and brothers and sisters and mothers and children and lands, with persecutions" (Mk 10:30). Judge not by appearance, but be sure that, even when things seem to brighten and smile upon God's true servants, there is much within to try them, though you see it not. Of old time they wore clothing of hair and sackcloth under rich robes. Men do not observe this custom today; but be quite sure still that there are as many sharp distresses underneath the visible garb of things as if they did. Many a secret ailment or scarcely-observed infirmity exercises him who has it better than thorns or knotted cord. Many an apprehension for the future which cannot be spoken; many a bereavement which has robbed the world's gifts of their pleasant savor and leads the heart but to sigh at the sight of them.

No, never while the Church lasts will the words of old Jacob be reversed. All things here are against us but God, but if God be for us, who can really be against us? If he is in the midst of us, how shall we be moved? If Christ has died and risen again, what death can come upon us, though we be made to die daily? What sorrow, pain, humiliation, trial, but must end as his has ended, in a continual resurrection into his new world and in a nearer and nearer approach to him? He pronounced a blessing over his apostles, and they have scattered it far and wide all over the earth unto this day. It runs as follows: "Peace I leave with you; my peace I give to you; not as the world gives do I give to you . . . . I have said this to you, that in me you may have peace. In the world you have tribulation; but be of good cheer, I have overcome the world" (Jn 14:27; Jn 16:33).

Palm Sunday

The Incarnate Son, a Sufferer and Sacrifice, I

He who humbled himself, being first made man, then dying, and that upon a shameful and agonizing cross, was the same who from eternity had been "in the form of God" and was equal to God, as the apostle declares (Phil 2:6). "In the beginning was the Word, and the Word was with God, and the Word was God. He was in the beginning with God" (Jn 1:1-2); thus speaks St. John, a second witness to the same great and awful truth. And he, too, goes on to say, "And the Word became flesh and dwelt among us" (Jn 1:14). And at the close of his Gospel, he gives an account of our Lord's death upon the Cross.

We are now approaching that most sacred day when we commemorate Christ's passion and death. Let us try to fix our minds upon this great thought. Let us try, what is so very difficult, to put off other thoughts, to clear our minds of things transitory, temporal, and earthly, and to occupy them with the contemplation of the Eternal Priest and his one ever-enduring sacrifice, that sacrifice which, though completed once for all on Calvary, yet ever abides, and, in its power and its grace, is ever present among us and is at all times gratefully and awfully to be commemorated, but now especially. Let us look upon him who was lifted up that he might draw us to him, and, by being drawn one and all to him, let us be drawn to each other, so that we may understand and feel that he has redeemed us one and all, and that, unless we love one another, we cannot really love him who laid down his life for us.

In the first place, then, it must be ever remembered that Christ's death was not a mere martyrdom. A martyr is one who dies for the Church, who is put to death for preaching and maintaining the truth. Christ, indeed, was put to death for preaching the gospel, yet he was not a martyr. He was much more than a martyr. Man dies as a martyr, but the Son of God dies as an atoning sacrifice.

It would be well if we opened our minds to what is meant by the doctrine of the Son of God dying on the Cross for us. The Almighty Son of God, who had been in the bosom of the Father from everlasting, became man, became man as truly as he was always God. He was God from God, as the Creed says, that is, as being the Son of the Father, he had all those infinite perfections from the Father which the Father had. He was of one substance with the Father, and was God, because the Father was God. He was truly God, but he became as truly man. He became man, yet so as not to cease in any respect being what he was before. He added a new nature to himself, yet so intimately that it was as if he had actually left his former self, which he did not. The word became flesh: even this would seem mystery and marvel enough, but even this was not all. Not only was he made man, but, as the Creed goes on to state, he was "crucified under Pontius Pilate, suffered, died, and was buried."

Here is a fresh mystery in the history of his humiliation. After his incarnation, man's nature was as much and as truly Christ's as his divine attributes. St. Paul even speaks of the "Lord of Glory" being "crucified" (1 Cor 2:8), an expression which, more than any other, shows how absolutely and simply he had put on him the nature of man. As the soul acts through the body as its instrument, in a more perfect way, but as intimately did the Eternal Word of God act through the manhood which he had taken. When he spoke, it was literally God speaking.

When he suffered, it was God suffering. Not that the divine nature itself could suffer, any more than our soul can see or hear, but as the soul sees and hears through the organs of the body, so God the Son suffered in that human nature which he had taken to himself and made his own. And in that nature he did truly suffer. As truly as he framed the worlds through his almighty power, so through his human nature did he suffer. For when he came on earth, his manhood became as truly and personally his as his almighty power had been from everlasting.

Think of this and consider whether with this thought you can read the last chapters of the four Gospels without fear and trembling.

For instance, "When he had said this, one of the officers standing by struck Jesus with his hand, saying, 'Is that how you answer the high priest?'" (Jn 18:22). The words must be said: that officer lifted up his hand against God the Son. This is not a figurative way of speaking, a rhetorical form of words, or a harsh, extreme, and unadvisable statement. It is a literal and simple truth. It is a great Catholic doctrine.

Again: "Then they spat in his face, and struck him; and some slapped him" (Mt 26:67).

"Now the men who were holding Jesus mocked him and beat him; they also blindfolded him and asked him, "Prophesy! Who is it that struck you?" And they spoke many other words against him, reviling him" (Lk 22:63-65).

"And Herod with his soldiers treated him with contempt and mocked him; then, clothing him in gorgeous apparel, he sent him back to Pilate" (Lk 23:11).

"Then Pilate took Jesus and scourged him. And the soldiers plaited a crown of thorns, and put it on his head, and clothed him in a purple robe; they came up to him, saying, 'Hail, King of the Jews!' and struck him with their hands. Pilate went out again, and said to them, 'Behold, I am bringing him out to you, that you may know that I find no crime in him.' So Jesus came out, wearing the crown of thorns and the purple robe" (Jn 19:1-5).

Lastly: "when they came to the place which is called The Skull, there they crucified him" (Lk 23:33) between two malefactors, and even there they did not cease insulting and mocking him, but all of them, chief priests and people, stood beholding and bidding him come down from the Cross.

Consider that that face, so ruthlessly smitten, was the face of God himself. The brows bloody with the thorns, the sacred body exposed to view and lacerated with the scourge, the hands nailed to the Cross, and, afterwards, the side pierced with the spear: it was the blood, and the temples, and the side, and the feet of God himself. This is so fearful a thought that when the mind first masters it, surely it will be difficult to think of anything else, so that, while we think of it, we must pray God to temper it to us and to give us strength to think of it rightly, lest it be too much for us.

Monday of Holy Week

The Incarnate Son, a Sufferer and Sacrifice, II

The sufferings and death of the Word Incarnate could not pass away like a dream. They could not be a mere martyrdom, or a mere display or figure of something else: they must have a virtue in them. This we might be sure of, though nothing had been told us about the result. But that result is also revealed. It is this: our reconciliation to God, the expiation of our sins, and our new creation in holiness.

We had need of a reconciliation for by nature we are outcasts. From the time that Adam fell, all his children have been under a curse. "In Adam all die" (1 Cor 15:22), as St. Paul says. Every one of us is born into this world in a state of death. Such is our natural life from our very first breath. We are children of wrath, conceived in sin, shaped in iniquity. We are under the bondage of an inborn element of evil, which thwarts and stifles whatever principles remain of truth and goodness in us, as soon as we attempt to act according to them. This is that "body of death" under which St. Paul describes the natural man as groaning, and saying, "Wretched man that I am! Who will deliver me?" (Rom 7:24). Now for ourselves, we know—praised be God—that all of us have from our infancy been taken out of this miserable heathen state by holy baptism, which is God's appointed means of regeneration. Still it is not less our natural state; it is the state in which everyone of us was born. It is the state in which every little child is when brought to the font. Dear as he is to those who bring him there, and innocent as he may look, there is, till he is baptized, an evil spirit in his heart, a spirit of evil lying hid, seen of God, unseen by man (as the serpent among the trees of Eden), an evil spirit which from the first bears hatred towards God and at length will be his eternal ruin. That evil spirit is cast out by holy baptism, without the privilege of which his birth would be but a misery to him. But whence did baptism gain its power? From that great event we are so soon to commemorate: the death of the Son of God incarnate.

Almost all religions have their outward cleansings; they feel the need of man, though they cannot supply it. Even the Jewish system, though divine, effected nothing here. Its washings were but carnal. The blood of bulls and goats was but earthly and unprofitable. Even St. John's baptism had no inward propitiatory power. Christ was not yet crucified. But when that long-expected season came, when the Son of God had solemnly set himself apart as a victim in the presence of his twelve apostles, and had gone into the garden, and before three of them had undergone his agony and bloody sweat, and then had been betrayed, buffeted, spit upon, scourged, and nailed to the Cross till he died, then he with his last breath said, "It is finished" (Jn 19:30): from that time the virtue of the Highest went forth through his wounds and with his blood for the pardon and regeneration of man. And hence it is that baptism has its power.

This is why he "humbled himself and became obedient unto death, even death on a cross" (Phil 2:8). "Christ redeemed us," says the apostle elsewhere, "from the curse of the law, having become a curse for us" (Gal 3:13). Again, he says that Christ has made "peace by the blood of his cross" (Col 1:20). He has "reconciled" us "in his body of flesh by his death, in order to present [us] holy and blameless and irreproachable before him" (Col 1:22). Or, as St. John says, the saints "washed their robes and made them white in the blood of the Lamb" (Rev 7:14). And no one speaks more explicitly on this great mystery than the prophet Isaiah, many hundred years before it was accomplished. "Surely he has borne our griefs and carried our sorrows; yet we esteemed him stricken, struck down by God, and afflicted. But he was wounded for our transgressions, he was bruised for our iniquities; upon him was the chastisement that made us whole, and with his stripes we are healed. All we like sheep have gone astray; we have turned every one to his own way; and the Lord has laid on him the iniquity of us all" (Is 53:4-6).

We believe, then, that when Christ suffered on the Cross, our nature suffered in him. Human nature, fallen and corrupt, was under the wrath of God, and it was impossible that it should be restored to his favor till it had expiated its sin by suffering. Why this was necessary, we know not; but we are told expressly that we are "by nature children of wrath" (Eph 2:3), that "no human being will be justified in his sight by works of the law" (Rom 3:20), and that the "wicked shall depart to Sheol, all the nations that forget God" (Ps 9:17). The Son of God then took our nature on him, that in him it might do and suffer what in itself was impossible to it. What it could not effect of itself, it could effect in him. He carried it about him through a life of penance. He carried it forward to agony and death. In him our sinful nature died and rose again. When it died in him on the Cross, that death was its new creation. In him it satisfied its old and heavy debt, for the presence of his divinity gave it transcendent merit. His presence had kept it pure from sin from the first. His hand had carefully selected the choicest specimen of our nature from the Virgin's substance, and, separating it from all defilement, his personal indwelling hallowed it and gave it power. And thus, when it had been offered up upon the Cross and was made perfect by suffering, it became the first-fruits of a new man. It became a divine leaven of holiness for the new birth and spiritual life of as many as should receive it. And thus, as the apostle says, "one has died for all; therefore all have died" (2 Cor 5:14); "our former man was crucified with him so that the sinful body might be destroyed" (Rom 6:6); and "when we were dead through our trespasses" he "made us alive together with Christ . . . and raised us up with him, and made us sit with him in the heavenly places in Christ Jesus" (Eph 2:5-6). Thus "we are members of his body" (Eph 5:30), from his flesh and from his bones. For whoever eats his flesh and drinks his blood "has eternal life," for his "flesh is food indeed" and his "blood is drink indeed" and he who eats his flesh and drinks his blood "abides" in him (see Jn 6:54-56).

Tuesday of Holy Week

The Mental Sufferings of Our Lord in His Passion, I

Our Lord and Savior, though he was God, was also perfect man; and hence he had not only a body, but a soul likewise, such as ours, though pure from all stain of evil. How would he have sanctified our nature by taking a nature which was not ours? Man without a soul is on a level with the beasts of the field; but our Lord came to save a race capable of praising and obeying him, possessed of immortality, though that immortality had lost its promised blessedness. Man was created in the image of God, and that image is in his soul. When then his Maker, by an unspeakable condescension, came in his nature, he took on himself a soul in order to take on him a body. He himself created the soul which he took on himself, while he took his body from the flesh of the Blessed Virgin, his Mother. Thus he became perfect man with body and soul, and as he took on him a body of flesh and nerves, which admitted of wounds and death and was capable of suffering, so did he take a soul, too, which was susceptible of that suffering, and moreover was susceptible of the pain and sorrow which are proper to a human soul. And, as his atoning passion was undergone in the body, so it was undergone in the soul also.

His sufferings in the body—his seizure, forced journeyings, blows and wounds, scourging, the crown of thorns, the nails—are all summed up in the crucifix. They are represented all at once on his sacred flesh, as it hangs up before us, and meditation is made easy by the spectacle. It is otherwise with the sufferings of his soul. They cannot be painted for us, nor can they even be duly investigated. They are beyond both sense and thought, and yet they anticipated his bodily sufferings. The agony, a pain of the soul, not of the body, was the first act of his tremendous sacrifice. "My soul is very sorrowful, even to death" (Mt 26:38), he said.

It was the soul and not the body which was the seat of the suffering of the Eternal Word. There is no real pain, though there may be apparent suffering, when there is no kind of inward sensibility or spirit to be the seat of it. A tree, for instance, has life, organs, growth, and decay; it may be wounded and injured; it droops, and is killed; but it does not suffer, because it has no mind or sensible principle within it. But wherever this gift of an immaterial principle is found, there pain is possible, and greater pain according to the quality of the gift. Had we no soul, we should not feel pain more acutely than a brute feels it; but, being men, we feel pain in a way in which none but those who have souls can feel it.

This it is what makes pain so trying: we cannot help thinking of it, while we suffer it. It is before us; it possesses the mind; it keeps our thoughts fixed upon it. Whatever draws the mind off the thought of it lessens it. Hence friends try to amuse us when we are in pain, for amusement is a diversion. And hence it continually happens that in violent exercise or labor, men meet with blows or cuts so considerable and so durable in their effect as to bear witness to the suffering which must have attended their infliction, of which nevertheless they recollect nothing. And in quarrels and in battles wounds are received which, from the excitement of the moment, are brought home to the consciousness of the combatant not by the pain at the time of receiving them but by the loss of blood that follows.

Hardly any one stroke of pain is intolerable; it is intolerable when it continues. Patients feel as if they could stop the surgeon's hand, simply because he continues to pain them. Their feeling is that they have borne as much as they can bear, as if the continuance and not the intensity was what made it too much for them. What does this mean, but that the memory of the foregoing moments of pain acts upon the pain that succeeds? If the third or fourth or twentieth moment of pain could be taken by itself, if the succession of the moments that preceded it could be forgotten, it would be no more than the first moment, as bearable as the first; but what makes it unbearable is that it is the twentieth. Hence it is that brute animals would seem to feel so little pain. They do not know they exist; they do not contemplate themselves; they do not look backwards or forwards; every moment as it succeeds is their all. And hence, as their other feelings, so their feeling of pain is but faint and dull, in spite of their outward manifestations of it. It is the intellectual comprehension of pain, as a whole diffused through successive moments, which gives it its special power and keenness.

Now apply this to the sufferings of our Lord. They offered him wine mingled with myrrh when he was on the point of being crucified, but he would not drink of it. Why? Because such a portion would have stupefied his mind, and he was bent on bearing the pain in all its bitterness. You see from this the character of his sufferings. He would have willingly escaped them had that been His Father's will. "If it be possible," he said, "let this chalice pass from me" (Mt 26:39), but since it was not possible, he says calmly and decidedly to the apostle, who would have rescued him from suffering, "shall I not drink the chalice which the Father has given me?" (Jn 18:11). If he was to suffer, he gave himself to suffering. And as men are superior to brute animals and are affected by pain more than they by reason of the mind within them, so, in like manner, our Lord felt pain of the body, with a consciousness, and therefore with a keenness and intensity, and with a unity of perception, which none of us can possibly fathom or compass, because his soul was so absolutely in his power, so simply free from the influence of distractions, so fully directed upon the pain, so utterly surrendered, so simply subjected to the suffering. And thus he may truly be said to have suffered the whole of his passion in every moment of it.

Recollect that our Blessed Lord was in this respect different from us, that, though he was perfect man, yet there was a power in him greater than his soul, which ruled his soul, for he was God. The soul of other men is subjected to its own wishes, feelings, impulses, passions, perturbations. His soul was subjected simply to his Eternal and Divine Personality. Nothing happened to his soul by chance or on a sudden. He never was taken by surprise. Nothing affected him without his willing beforehand that it should. When we suffer, it is because outward agents and the uncontrollable emotions of our minds bring suffering upon us. We are brought under the discipline of pain involuntarily. We suffer from it more or less acutely according to accidental circumstances. We find our patience more or less tried by it according to our state of mind, and we do our best to provide alleviations or remedies of it. We cannot anticipate beforehand how much of it will come upon us, or how far we shall be able to sustain it; nor can we say afterwards why we have felt just what we have felt, or why we did not bear the suffering better.

It was otherwise with our Lord. His Divine Person was not subject to the influence of his own human affections and feelings, except so far as he chose. He was not open to emotion, but he opened upon himself voluntarily the impulse by which he was moved. Consequently, when he determined to suffer the pain of his vicarious passion, whatever he did, he did not do it by halves. He did not turn away his mind from the suffering as we do. He said, "sacrifices and offerings you have not desired, but a body you have prepared for me" (Heb 10:5). He took a body in order that he might suffer. He became man, that he might suffer as man, and when his hour was come, that hour of Satan and of darkness, the hour when sin was to pour its full malignity upon him, it followed that he offered himself wholly; as the whole of his body, stretched out upon the Cross, so the whole of his soul, his whole consciousness, a mind awake, a sense acute, a living cooperation, a present, absolute intention, not a virtual permission, not a heartless submission, this did he present to his tormentors. His passion was an action. He lived most energetically while he lay languishing, fainting, and dying. Nor did he die except by an act of the will, for he bowed his head, in command as well as in resignation, and said, "Father, into your hands I commend my Spirit" (Lk 23:46).

Had our Lord only suffered in the body, and in it not so much as other men, still as regards the pain, he would have really suffered indefinitely more, because pain is to be measured by the power of realizing it. God was the sufferer. God suffered in his human nature. The sufferings belonged to God, and were drunk up, were drained out to the bottom of the chalice, because God drank them; not tasted or sipped, not flavored, disguised by human medicaments, as man disposes of the cup of anguish.

Wednesday of Holy Week

The Mental Sufferings of Our Lord in His Passion, II

Our Lord said, when his agony was commencing, "My soul is very sorrowful, even to death" (Mt 26:38); now we may ask whether he had not certain consolations peculiar to himself, impossible in any other, which diminished or impeded the distress of his soul, and caused him to feel, not more, but less than an ordinary man. For instance, he had a sense of innocence which no other sufferer could have; even his persecutors, even the false apostle who betrayed him, the judge who sentenced him, and the soldiers who conducted the execution, testified his innocence. And if even they, sinners, bore witness to his sinlessness, how much more did his own soul! And we know well that even in our own case, sinners as we are, on the consciousness of innocence or of guilt mainly turns our power of enduring opposition and calumny; how much more in the case of our Lord, did the sense of inward sanctity compensate for the suffering and annihilate the shame. Again, he knew that his sufferings would be short, and that their issue would be joyful, whereas uncertainty of the future is the keenest element of human distress; but he could not have anxiety, for he was not in suspense; nor despondency or despair, for he never was deserted. And in confirmation you may refer to St. Paul, who expressly tells us that, "for the joy that was set before him," our Lord "endured the cross, despising the shame" (Heb 12:2). And certainly there is a marvelous calm and self-possession in all he does.

He was always himself. His mind was its own center and was never in the slightest degree thrown off its heavenly and most perfect balance. What he suffered, he suffered because he put himself under suffering, and that deliberately and calmly. His composure is but the proof how entirely he governed his own mind. He drew back, at the proper moment, the bolts and fastenings, and opened the gates, and the floods fell right upon his soul in all their fullness. That is what St. Mark tells us of him; and he is said to have written his Gospels from the very mouth of St. Peter, who was one of three witnesses present at the time.

"And they went to a place which was called Gethsemane; and he said to his disciples, 'Sit here, while I pray.' And he took with him Peter and James and John, and began to be greatly distressed and troubled" (Mk 14:32-33). Thus he walks forth into a mental agony with as definite an action as if it were some bodily torture, the fire or the wheel.

It is nothing to the purpose to say that he would be supported under his trial by the consciousness of innocence and the anticipation of triumph; for his trial consisted in the withdrawal, as of other causes of consolation, so of that very consciousness and anticipation. The same act of the will which admitted the influence upon his soul of any distress at all, admitted all distresses at once. It was not the contest between antagonist impulses and views, coming from without, but the operation of an inward resolution. As men of self-command can turn from one thought to another at their will, so much more did he deliberately deny himself the comfort and satiate himself with the woe.

What was it he had to bear when he thus opened upon his soul the torrent of this predestinated pain? Alas! He had to bear what is well known to us, what is familiar to us, but what to him was woe unutterable. He had to bear the weight of sin. He had to bear our sins. He had to bear the sins of the whole world. Sin is an easy thing to us; we think little of it. We do not understand how the Creator can think much of it. We cannot bring our imagination to believe that it deserves retribution. But consider what sin is in itself. It is rebellion against God. Sin is the mortal enemy of the All-holy. And here observe that when once Almighty Love, by taking flesh, entered this created system, and submitted himself to its laws, then forthwith this antagonist of good and truth, taking advantage of the opportunity, flew at that flesh which he had taken, and fixed on it, and was its death. The envy of the Pharisees, the treachery of Judas, and the madness of the people were but the instrument or the expression of the enmity which sin felt towards Eternal Purity as soon as, in infinite mercy towards men, he put himself within its reach. Sin could not touch his Divine Majesty, but it could assail him in that way in which he allowed himself to be assailed, that is, through the medium of his humanity.

In that most awful hour, there knelt the Savior of the world, putting off the defenses of his divinity, dismissing his reluctant angels, who in myriads were ready at his call, and opening his arms, baring his breast, sinless as he was, to the assault of his foe. There he knelt, motionless and still, while the vile and horrible fiend clad his spirit in a robe steeped in all that is hateful and heinous in human crime, which clung close round his heart, and filled his conscience, and found its way into every sense and pore of his mind and spread over him a moral leprosy. Oh, the horror, when he looked and did not know himself, and felt as a foul and loathsome sinner, from his vivid perception of that mass of corruption which poured over his head and ran down even to the skirts of his garments! Oh, the distraction, when he found his eyes, and hands, and feet, and lips, and heart, as if the members of the Evil One and not of God! Are these the hands of the Immaculate Lamb of God, once innocent, but now red with ten thousand barbarous deeds of blood? Are these his lips, not uttering prayer, and praise, and holy blessings, but as if defiled with oaths, and blasphemies, and doctrines of devils? Or his eyes, profaned by all the evil visions and idolatrous fascinations for which men have abandoned their adorable Creator? And his ears, they ring with sounds of revelry and of strife; and his heart is frozen with avarice, and cruelty, and unbelief. His very memory is laden with every sin which has been committed since the fall.

Who does not know the misery of a haunting thought which comes again and again, in spite of rejection, to annoy, if it cannot seduce? Or of some odious and sickening imagination, in no sense one's own, but forced upon the mind from without? Or of evil knowledge, gained with or without a man's fault, but which he would give a great price to be rid of at once and for ever? And adversaries such as these gather around you, Blessed Lord, in millions now. Of the living and of the dead and of the as yet unborn, of the lost and of the saved, of your people and of strangers, of sinners and of saints, all sins are there. Your dearest are there, your saints and your chosen are upon you, your three apostles, Peter, James, and John, but not as comforters, but as accusers, heaping curses on your head. All are there but one. One only is not there, one only, for she who had no part in sin, she only could console you, and therefore she is not nigh. She will be near you on the Cross, she is separated from you in the garden. None was equal to the weight but God. It is the long history of a world, and God alone can bear the load of it. Hopes blighted, vows broken, lights quenched, warnings scorned, opportunities lost; the innocent betrayed, the young hardened, the penitent relapsing, the just overcome, the aged failing; the sophistry of misbelief, the willfulness of passion, the obduracy of pride, the tyranny of habit, the canker of remorse, the wasting fever of care, the anguish of shame, the pining of disappointment, the sickness of despair. Such cruel, such pitiable spectacles, such heartrending, revolting, detestable, maddening scenes: they are all before him now. They are upon him and in him. They are with him instead of that ineffable peace which has inhabited his soul since the moment of his conception. They are upon him. They are all but his own. He cries to his Father as if he were the criminal, not the victim. His agony takes the form of guilt and compunction. He is doing penance. He is making confession. He is exercising contrition, with a reality and a virtue infinitely greater than that of all saints and penitents together, for he is the One Victim for us all, the sole Satisfaction, the real Penitent, all but the real sinner.

He rises languidly from the earth and turns around to meet the traitor and his band, now quickly nearing the deep shade. He turns, and lo there is blood upon his garment. No soldier's scourge has touched his shoulders, nor the hangman's nails his hands and feet. He has bled before his time. He has shed blood, and it is his agonizing soul which has broken up his framework of flesh and poured it forth. His passion has begun from within. That tormented heart, the seat of tenderness and love, began at length to labor and to beat with vehemence beyond its nature. The red streams rushed forth so copious and fierce as to overflow the veins, and bursting through the pores, they stood in a thick dew over his whole skin. Then, forming into drops, they rolled down full and heavy, and drenched the ground.

Holy Thursday

Knowledge of God's Will

To us our Savior says, "If you know these things, blessed are you if you do them" (Jn 13:17). Let us try, by his grace, to make this saying a living word to the benefit of our souls. Let us consider, in its light, how we commonly read Scripture.

We read a passage in the Gospels, for instance a parable or the account of a miracle, or we read a chapter in the Prophets, or a Psalm. Who is not struck by the beauty of what he reads? Take the passage that introduces this saying. Christ had been washing his disciples' feet. He did so at a season of great mental suffering; it was just before he was seized by his enemies to be put to death. The traitor, his familiar friend, was in the room. All of his disciples, even the most devoted of them, loved him much less than they thought they did. In a little while, they were all to forsake him and flee. This he foresaw, yet he calmly washed their feet, and then he told them that he did so by way of an example: that they should be full of lowly services one to the other as he to them; that he among them was in fact the highest who put himself the lowest. This he had said before, and his disciples must have recollected it. Perhaps they might wonder in their secret hearts why he repeated the lesson. They might say to themselves, "We have heard this before." They might be surprised that his significant action, his washing their feet, issued in nothing else than a precept already delivered, the command to be humble. At the same time, they would not be able to deny, or rather they would deeply feel, the beauty of his action. As loving him above all things, and reverencing him as their lord and teacher, they would feel an admiration and awe of him. But their minds would not rest sufficiently on the practical direction of the instruction given to them. They knew the truth, and they admired it; they did not observe what it was they lacked. Such may be considered their frame of mind. Hence the force of the saying, which was delivered primarily against Judas Iscariot, who knew and sinned deliberately against the truth, but secondarily referring to all the apostles and to St. Peter chiefly, who promised to be faithful but failed under the trial, and lastly to us all, who hear the word of life continually, know it, admire it, do all but obey it.

Is it not so? Is not Scripture altogether pleasant except in its strictness? Do we not try to persuade ourselves that to feel religiously, to confess our love of religion, to be able to talk of religion will stand in the place of careful obedience and self-denial? Alas, that a religion which is do delightful as a vision should be so distasteful to us as a reality.

But if you are really pierced to the heart that you do not do what you know you should do, then the Gospel speaks to you words of peace and hope. It is a very different thing indolently to say, "I wish I were a different man," and to accept God's offer to make you different when it is put before you. Here is the test between earnestness and insincerity. You say you wish to be a different man. Christ takes you at your word; he offers to make you different. He says, "I will take away from you the heart of stone, the love of this world and its pleasures, if you will submit to the love of my discipline." Here a man draws back. He cannot bear to lose the love of the world, to part with his present desires and tastes. He cannot consent to be changed.

But if a man is in earnest in wishing to get at the depths of his own heart, to expel the evil, to purify the good, and to gain power over himself so as to do as well as know the truth, what is the difficulty? So simple is the rule which he must follow that at first he will be surprised to hear it. God does great things by plain methods, and men are surprised by them through pride because they are plain. Christ says, "Watch and pray" (Mt 26:41). Herein lies our cure. To watch and pray are surely in our power, and by these means we are certain of getting strength.

You fear your weakness; you fear to be overcome by temptation. Then keep out of the way of it. This is watching. Avoid society which is likely to mislead you. Flee from the very shadow of evil. Better to be a little too strict than a little too easy: it is the safer side. Abstain from reading books which are dangerous to you. Turn from bad thoughts when they arise. Set about some business, begin conversing with a friend, or say to yourself the Lord's Prayer reverently. When you are urged by temptation, whether it be by the threats of the world, false shame, self-interest, provoking conduct on the part of another, or the world's sinful pleasures, urged to be cowardly, or covetous, or unforgiving, or sensual, shut your eyes and think of Christ's precious blood-shedding. Do not dare to say you cannot help sinning. A little attention to these points will go far—through God's grace—to keep you in the right way.

Again, pray as well as watch. You must know that you can do nothing of yourself. Your past experience has taught you this. Therefore, look to God for the will and the power. Ask him earnestly in his Son's name. Seek his holy ordinances. Is not this in your power? Have you not power at least over the limbs of your body so as to attend the means of grace constantly? Have you literally not the power to observe the fasts and festivals of the Church, to come to his holy altar and receive the Bread of Life? Get yourself, at least, to do this: to receive his precious Body and Blood. This is no arduous work. What would you have more than a free gift, given "without money and without price"? (Is 55:1). So, make no more excuses. Murmur not about your own bad heart, your knowing and resolving but not doing. Here is your remedy.

Good Friday

The Crucifixion

St. Peter makes it almost a description of a Christian that he loves him whom he has not seen. Speaking of Christ, he says, "without having seen him you love him; though you do not now see him you believe in him and rejoice with unutterable and exalted joy" (1 Pet 1:8). Again, he speaks of tasting "the kindness of the Lord" (1 Pet 2:3). Unless we have a true love of Christ, we are not his true disciples, and we cannot love him unless we have heartfelt gratitude to him, and we cannot duly feel gratitude, unless we feel keenly what he suffered for us. It seems impossible that anyone can have attained to the love of Christ who feels no distress, no misery, at the thought of his bitter pains, and no self-reproach at having through his own sins had a share in causing them.

Feeling is not enough. It is not enough merely to feel and nothing more. To feel grief for Christ's sufferings and yet not to go on to obey him is not true love, but a mockery. True love both feels right and acts right. At the same time as warm feelings without religious conduct are a kind of hypocrisy, so also right conduct, when unattended by deep feelings, is at best a very imperfect sort of religion. And on this day, especially are we called upon to raise our hearts to Christ and to have keen feelings and piercing thoughts of sorrow and shame, of compunction and of gratitude, of love and tender affection and horror and anguish, at the review of those awful sufferings whereby our salvation has been purchased.

Let us pray God to give us all graces. And while, in the first place, we pray that he would make us holy, really holy, let us also pray him to give us the beauty of holiness, which consists in tender and eager affection towards our Lord and Savior, so that through God's mercy our souls may have not strength and health only but a sort of bloom and comeliness, and that as we grow older in body, we may, year by year, grow more youthful in spirit.

As to his sufferings, we know that our Lord is called a lamb, that is, he was as defenseless and as innocent as a lamb is. And this was just our Savior's case. He had laid aside his glory. He had, as it were, disbanded his legions of angels. He came on earth without arms, except the arms of truth, meekness, and righteousness, and committed himself to the world in perfect innocence and sinlessness, and in utter helplessness. In the words of St. Peter, "He committed no sin; no guile was found on his lips. When he was reviled, he did not revile in return; when he suffered, he did not threaten; but he trusted to him who judges justly" (1 Pet 2:22-23). He who is higher than the angels deigned to humble himself even to the state of the brute creation, as the Psalm says, "I am a worm, and no man; scorned by men, and despised by the people" (Ps 22:6).

Think of him, when in his wounded state, and without garment on, he had to creep up the ladder, as best he could, which led him up the Cross high enough for his murderers to nail him to it, and consider who it was that was in that misery. Or again, view him dying, hour after hour bleeding to death, and how? In peace? No. With his arms stretched out, and his face exposed to view, and anyone who pleased coming and staring at him, mocking him, and watching the gradual ebbing of his strength and the approach of death. These are some of the appalling details which the Gospels contain, and surely they were not recorded for nothing, but that we might dwell on them.

Do you think that those who saw these things had much heart for eating or drinking or enjoying themselves? On the contrary, we are told that even "the multitudes who assembled to see the sight, when they saw what had taken place, returned home beating their breasts" (Lk 23:48). If these were the feelings of the people, what were St. John's feelings, or St. Mary Magdalene's, or St. Mary's, our Lord's blessed mother? Do we desire to be of their company? Do we desire to be as his brother, and sister, and mother? Then, surely, ought we to have some portion of that mother's sorrow.

It is said in the Book of Revelation, "Behold, he is coming with the clouds, and every eye will see him, every one who pierced him; and all tribes of the earth will wail on account of him" (Rev 1:7). We shall one day rise from our graves and see Jesus Christ. We shall see him who hung on the Cross. We shall see his wounds, the marks in his hands, in his feet, and in his side. Do we wish to be one of those, then, who wail and lament, or of those who rejoice? If we would not lament at the sight of him then, we must lament at the thought of him now. Let us prepare to meet our God. Let us come into his presence whenever we can. Let us try to fancy as if we saw the Cross and him upon it. Let us draw near to it. Let us beg him to look on us as he did on the penitent thief, and let us say to him, "Jesus, remember me when you come in your kingly power" (Lk 23:42), that is, "Remember me, Lord, in mercy, remember not my sins, but your cross; remember your sufferings, remember that you suffered for me, a sinner; remember in the last day that I, during my lifetime, felt your sufferings, that I suffered on the Cross by your side. Remember me then, and make me remember you now."

Holy Saturday

Moses, a Type of Christ

The history of Moses is valuable, not only as giving us a pattern of fidelity towards God, of great firmness, and great meekness, but also as affording us a type or figure of our Savior Christ. No prophet arose in Israel like Moses, till Christ came, when the promise was fulfilled: "the Lord your God will raise up for you a prophet like me" (Deut 18:15).

If we survey the general history of the Israelites, we shall find that it is a picture of man's history, as the dispensation of the Gospel displays it to us, and that in it Moses takes the place of Christ. The Israelites were in the land of strangers, the Egyptians. They were slaves, given heavy labor and wretched, and God broke their bonds and led them out of Egypt, after many perils, to the promised land, a land flowing with milk and honey. How clearly this prefigures to us the condition of the Christian Church. We are by nature in a strange country. God was our first Father, and his presence our dwelling place, but we were cast out of paradise for sinning and are in a dreary land, a valley of darkness and the shadow of death. We are born in this spiritual Egypt, the land of strangers. Still we have old recollections about us and broken traditions of our original happiness and dignity as freemen. Thoughts come across us from time to time which show that we were born for better things than to be slaves. Yet by nature slaves we are, slaves to the devil. He is our hard task-master, as Pharaoh oppressed the Israelites. So much the worse than he, in that his chains, though we do not see them, become more and more heavy every year. They cling about us and grow. They multiply themselves. They shoot out and spread forth and encircle us, those chains of sin, with many links, weighing us down to earth till at last we are mere slaves of the soil, slaves of that fearful harvest which is eternal death. Satan is a tyrant over us, and it seems to us useless to rebel. If we attempt it, we are but overpowered by his huge might and his oppressive rule, and are made twice the children of hell that we were before. We may groan and look about, but we cannot fly from his country. Such is our state by nature.

But Moses conducted the Israelites from the house of bondage to their own land, from which their fathers had descended to Egypt. He came to them from God, and, armed with God's power, he smote their cruel enemies, led them out of Pharaoh's territory, divided the Red Sea, carried them through it, and at length brought them to the borders of Canaan. And who is it that has done this for us Christians? Who but the Eternal Son of God, our Lord and Savior, whose name in consequence we bear? He has rescued us from the arm of him who was stronger than we, and therefore Christ is a second Moses and a greater. Christ has broken the power of the devil. He leads us forth on our way and makes a path through all difficulties that we may go forward towards heaven.

Most men who have deliberately turned their hearts to seek God must recollect times when the view of the difficulties which lay before them and of their own weakness nearly made them sink through fear. Then they were like the children of Israel on the shore of the Red Sea. How boisterous did the waves look! And they could not see beyond them. They seemed taken by their enemies as in a net. Pharaoh with his horsemen hurried on to reclaim his runaway slaves. The Israelites sunk down in terror on the sand of the seashore. Every moment brought death or captivity nearer to them. Then it was that Moses said, "stand firm, and see the salvation of the Lord" (Ex 14:13).

In like manner has Christ spoken to us. When our hearts fainted within us, when we said to ourselves, "How is it possible that we should attain heaven?" When we felt how desirable it was to serve God but felt keenly the power of temptation. When we acknowledged in our hearts that God was holy and most adorable and obedience to his will most lovely and admirable, and yet recollected instances of our past disobedience and feared lest all our renewed resolutions to serve him would be broken and swept away by the old Adam as mercilessly as heretofore, and that Satan would regain us, and yet prayed earnestly to God for his saving help. Then he saved us from our fear, surprising us by the strangeness of our salvation. It happens to Christians not once, but again and again through life. Troubles are lightened, trials are surmounted, fears disappear. We are enabled to do things above our strength by trusting in Christ. We overcome our most urgent sins; we surrender our most innocent wishes; we conquer ourselves. We make a way through the powers of the world, the flesh, and the devil. The waves divide, and our Lord, the great captain of our salvation, leads us over. Christ, then, is a second Moses, and greater than he, inasmuch as Christ leads from hell to heaven.

Awake, then, with this season, to meet your God, who now summons you from his cross and tomb. Put aside the sin that so easily besets you and be holy even as he is holy. Stand ready to suffer with him, should it be needful, that you may rise together with him. He can make bitter things sweet to you and hard ways easy, if you have but the heart to desire him to do so. He can change the Law into the Gospel. He can, for Moses, give you himself.

Solemnity of St. Joseph

The Work of the Christian

Though God created the heavens and the earth in six days and then rested, yet he rested only to begin a work of another kind, for our Lord says, "my Father is working still," and he adds, "and I am working" (Jn 5:17). And at another time he says, concerning himself more expressly, "We must work the works of him who sent me, while it is day; night comes, when no one can work" (Jn 9:4). And when that night came, he said, "I glorified you on earth, having accomplished the work which you gave me to do" (Jn 17:4), and, "It is finished" (Jn 19:30). And we are told generally of all of us that "Man goes forth to his work and to his labor until the evening" (Ps 104:23). The Creator wrought till the Sabbath came; the Redeemer wrought till the sun was darkened and it was night. In the evening, man returns to God, and his works, whether good or whether evil, do follow him.

This solemn truth, that we are sent here to do a work, is set before us in various ways. We read that Adam was placed in Paradise, the garden of Eden, "to till it and keep it" (Gen 2:15). Soon, alas, did he fall and become subject to heavier toil, the earth being cursed for his sake and bringing forth for him thorns and thistles. God, however, in his mercy, did not desert him, and, accordingly, we read in the Gospel of the householder going out from morning till evening "to hire laborers for his vineyard" (Mt 20:1). He went out early, and then about the third hour, and about the sixth and ninth, nor stopped till the eleventh. Such were his dealings with the race of men till the fullness of time was come, and in the last days, even at the eleventh hour, he sent his Son to gather together laborers for his work from all parts of the earth. And the history of those fresh gospel laborers is presented to us in the pattern of St. Paul, who served as a soldier, who planted a vineyard, who ploughed and thrashed and trod out the corn (see 1 Cor 9:7), for necessity was laid on him, and it was woe to him if he preached not the Gospel (see 1 Cor 9:16).

Oh, may we ever bear in mind that we are not sent into this world to stand all the day idle, but to go forth to our work and to our labor until the evening! Until the evening, not in the evening only of life, but serving God from our youth and not waiting till our years fail us. Until the evening, not in the day-time only, lest we begin to run well but fall away before our course is ended. Let us "give glory to the Lord [our] God before he brings darkness, before [our] feet stumble on the twilight mountains" (Jer 13:16), and, having turned to him, let us see that our goodness be not "like the morning mist or like the dew that goes early away" (Hos 13:3). The end is the proof of the matter. When the sun shines, this earth pleases, but let us look towards that eventide and the cool of the day when the Lord of the vineyard will walk amid the trees of his garden and say unto his steward, "Call the laborers and pay them their wages, beginning with the last, up to the first" (Mt 20:8). That evening will be the trial: when the heat, and fever, and noise of the noontide are over, and the light fades, and the prospect saddens, and the shades lengthen, and the busy world is still, and "the doors on the street are shut . . . and all the daughters of song are brought low . . . and terrors are in the way; the almond tree blossoms, the grasshopper drags itself along and desire fails" (Eccles 12:4-5), then, when it is "vanities of vanities, all is vanity" (Eccles 1:2), and the Lord shall come, "who will bring to light the things now hidden in darkness and will disclose the purposes of the heart" (1 Cor 4:5), then we shall discern "between the righteous and the wicked, between one who serves God and one who does not serve him" (Mal 3:18).

May that day and that hour ever be in our thoughts. When we rise, when we lie down, when we speak, when we are silent, when we act, and when we rest: whether we eat or drink, or whatever we do, may we never forget that "for all these things God will bring [us] into judgment" (Eccles 11:9). For he says, "I am coming soon, bringing my recompense, to repay every one for what he has done" (Rev 22:12).

"Blessed are those who wash their robes, that they may have the right to the tree of life and that they may enter the city by the gates" (Rev 22:14). Blessed will they be then, and only they, who, with the apostle, have ever had on their lips and in their hearts the question "Lord, what will you have me do?" (see Acts 9:6 in the KJV), whose soul has been "consumed with longing" for his ordinances (Ps 119:20) and who have hastened and did not delay in keeping his commandments (see Ps 119:60), who have not waited to be hired, but set themselves vigorously to do God's will.

Let us turn from shadows of all kinds, shadows of sense, or shadows of argument and disputation, or shadows addressed to our imagination and tastes. Let us attempt, through God's grace, to advance and sanctify the inward man. We cannot be wrong here. Whatever is right, whatever is wrong, in this perplexing world, we must be right in doing justly, in loving mercy, and in walking humbly with our God (see Mic 6:8), in denying our wills, in ruling our tongues, in softening and sweetening our tempers, in mortifying our desires, in learning patience, meekness, purity, forgiveness of injuries, and continuance in well-doing.

Solemnity of the Annunciation

The Incarnation

The Word was from the beginning, the only-begotten Son of God. Before all worlds were created, while as yet time was not, he was in existence, in the bosom of the Eternal Father, God from God, and Light from Light, supremely blessed in knowing and being known of him, and receiving all divine perfections from him, yet ever one with him who begat him. As it is said in the opening of St. John's Gospel: "In the beginning was the Word, and the Word was with God, and the Word was God" (Jn 1:1). If we may dare conjecture, he is called the Word of God, as mediating between the Father and all creatures, bringing them into being, fashioning them, giving the world its laws, imparting reason and conscience to creatures of a higher order, and revealing to them in due season the knowledge of God's will. And to us Christians, he is especially the Word in that great mystery commemorated today, whereby he became flesh and redeemed us from a state of sin.

He, indeed, when men fell, might have remained in the glory which he had with the Father before the world was. Yet that unsearchable love which showed itself in our original creation rested not content with a frustrated work but brought him down again from his Father's bosom to do his will and repair the evil which sin had caused. And with a wonderful condescension, he came not as before in power, but in weakness, in the form of a servant, in the likeness of that fallen creature whom he purposed to restore. So he humbled himself, suffering all the infirmities of our nature in the likeness of sinful flesh, all but a sinner—pure from all sin, yet subjected to temptation—and at length becoming obedient unto death, even the death of the Cross.

When the only-begotten Son stooped to take upon him our nature, he had no fellowship with sin. It was impossible that he should. Therefore, because our nature was corrupt since Adam's fall, he did not come in the way of nature. He did not clothe himself in that corrupt flesh which Adam's race inherits. He came by miracle, so as to take on him our imperfection without having any share in our sinfulness. He was not born as other men are, for "that which is born of the flesh is flesh" (Jn 3:6).

All Adam's children are children of wrath, so our Lord came as the Son of Man, but not the son of sinful Adam. He had no earthly father. He came by a new and living way; not, indeed, formed out of the ground, as Adam was at the first, lest he should miss the participation of our nature, but selecting and purifying unto himself a tabernacle out of that which existed. As in the beginning, woman was formed out of man by Almighty power, so now, by a like mystery, but a reverse order, the new Adam was fashioned from the woman. He was, as had been foretold, the immaculate seed of the woman (see Gen 3:15), deriving his manhood from the substance of the Virgin Mary.

Thus the Son of God became the Son of Man: mortal, but not a sinner; heir of our infirmities, not of our guilt; the offspring of the old race, yet the beginning of the new creation of God. Mary, his mother, was set apart, as "a garden locked, a fountain sealed" (Song 4:12), to yield a created nature to him who was her Creator. Thus he came into this world, not in the clouds of heaven, but born into it, born of a woman. He, the Son of Mary, and she, the mother of God. Thus he came, selecting and setting apart for himself the elements of body and soul, then, uniting them to himself from their first origin of existence, pervading them, hallowing them by his own divinity, filling them with light and purity, the while they continued to be human and for a time mortal and exposed to infirmity. And, as they grew from day to day in their holy union, his eternal essence was still one with them, exalting them, acting in them, manifesting itself through them, so that he was truly God and man, one person. As we are soul and body yet one man, so truly God and man are not two, but one Christ. Thus did the Son of God enter this mortal world. And when he had reached man's estate, he began his ministry, preached the Gospel, chose his apostles, suffered on the Cross, died, and was buried, rose again and ascended on high, there to reign till the day when he comes again to judge the world. This is the all-gracious mystery of the incarnation, good to look into, good to adore.

Let us then, according to the light given to us, praise and bless him in the Church below, whom angels in heaven see and adore. Let us bless him for his surpassing loving-kindness in taking upon him our infirmities to redeem us, when he dwelt in the innermost love of the everlasting Father, in the glory which he had with him before the world was. He came in lowliness and want, born amid the tumults of a mixed and busy multitude, cast aside into the out-building of a crowded inn, laid to his first rest among the brute cattle. He grew up, as if the native of a despised city, and was bred to a humble craft. He bore to live in a world that slighted him, for he lived in it in order in due time to die for it. He came as the appointed priest, to offer sacrifice for those who took no part in the act of worship. He came to offer up for sinners that precious blood which was meritorious by virtue of his divine anointing. He died, to rise again the third day, the sun of righteousness, fully displaying that splendor which had hitherto been concealed by the morning clouds. He rose again, to ascend to the right hand of God, there to plead his sacred wounds in token of our forgiveness, to rule and guide his ransomed people, and from his pierced side to pour forth his choicest blessings upon them. He ascended, thence to descend again in due season to judge the world which he has redeemed. Great is our Lord, and great is his power, Jesus, the Son of God and Son of man.

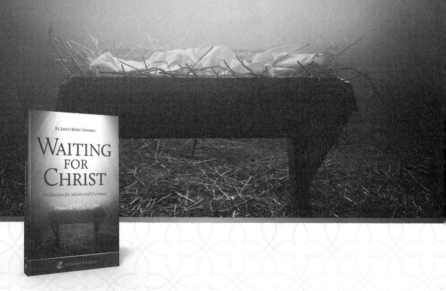

The Catholic Faith. On Demand.

Supporting an authentic Catholic lifestyle.

With thousands of Catholic movies, children's programs, e-books, audio talks, and Bible studies direct to your browser, mobile device, or connected TV, FORMED provides the very best Catholic content to help families and individuals explore their faith.

Sign up today for a FREE 7-day trial at **FORMED.org**.